napa bulletin

14

T0355713

Practicing Anthropology in Corporate America: Consulting on Organizational Culture

■ Ann T. Jordan, ed.

National Association for the Practice of Anthropology
A section of the American Anthropological Association

NAPA Bulletins are occasional publications of the National Association for the Practice of Anthropology, a section of the American Anthropological Assocition.

Ralph J. Bishop and Pamela Amoss
General Editors

Library of Congress Cataloging-in-Publication Data

Practicing anthropology in corporate America: consulting on organizational
culture / Ann T. Jordan, ed.
    p.   cm.—(NAPA bulletin ; 14)
    Includes bibliographical references.
    ISBN 0-913167-64-9
    1. Corporate culture. 2. Business anthropology. 3. Business consultants.
4. Anthropology—Vocational guidance.   I. Jordan, Ann. II. Series.
HD58.7.P7   1994
302.3'5—dc20   94-8980
                                                                    CIP

ISBN 0-913167-64-9

Contents

To the memory of Frank Dubinskas, whose research and writing included a decade of work on the interface of technology, organizations, and culture.

Introduction

For business anthropologists, the significance of the *organizational culture* concept in management consulting cannot be underestimated. The term has received so much popular press that it is known to business people at all levels throughout the country. The term in essence represents an anthropological approach to managing organizations and an area of analysis in which anthropologists are the experts. Thus the field is a natural for practitioners, and management consulting has opened up as one of the major growth fields for anthropologists in the 1990s. This bulletin provides a broad view of current research and consulting on organizational culture. It brings together anthropologists working in consulting and in departments of management, marketing, organizational behavior, family medicine, and anthropology to provide a varied perspective. On one level this bulletin is a how-to book for anthropologists interested in developing a consulting business on organizational culture. It includes tips on getting into consulting, advice on how to communicate with managers, and detailed examples of consulting work. It should be read as a companion to Giovannini and Rosansky's 1990 NAPA bulletin on management consulting, as that volume provides additional useful information not repeated here. On another level, this bulletin addresses conceptual questions of interest to all anthropologists. It integrates the conceptual basis of anthropology with the conceptual basis of management studies and discusses ways in which practice can influence theory in anthropology.

The bulletin is divided into two sections. The first section consists of two articles that give an overview of the conceptual framework of organizational culture. They discuss the relation between theory and practice and are designed to explain the relevant paradigms for consulting work. The second section of the bulletin is composed of a series of empirical studies. In each case the author defines organizational culture in the way she or he finds most utilitarian. Each includes a definition of organizational culture and an empirical example of its use. The cases are purposely diverse to provide the reader with a number of options in applying organizational culture in consulting.

If the reader is a new consultant, the chapters in this bulletin are of use in two ways. First, they provide examples of how to go about consulting on organizational culture. Second, they provide you with content to use in developing your own specialty. For example, you may want to adapt one of the definitions of organizational culture for your own use, or you may want to cite Kanu Kogod's statistics on diversity or Jill Kleinberg's descriptions of the difference between Japanese and American work sketch maps to demonstrate your own expertise to managers. Third, all the chapters, especially Nancy and Robert Morey's, give good insight into the worldview of managers, so that you can develop the ability to communicate your expertise effectively.

References Cited

Giovannini, Maureen J., and Lynne M. H. Rosansky
    1990   Anthropology and Management Consulting: Forging a New Alliance. NAPA Bulletin, 9. Washington, DC: American Anthropological Association.

Introducing the Concept

Organizational Culture: The Anthropological Approach

Ann T. Jordan

This chapter provides an overview of anthropology and organizational culture consulting. It discusses practical issues for consultants such as how to define organizational culture, what method and theory in anthropology to use in doing consulting, and what literature is available in anthropology. It also discusses theoretical and ethical issues that this work raises for all anthropologists, such as whether organizational culture is an appropriate use of the anthropological concept of culture and whether this work is ethical for anthropologists to perform. These are issues typical of the new era in anthropology in which models of culture and ethical guidelines are changing. Their solutions demonstrate contributions practice can make to traditional anthropology.

The Anthropological Literature

The term *organizational culture* has become popular in both anthropology and management over the last ten years. On the surface it appeared that the early clamor among business analysts regarding culture in organizations was largely a result of the American response to Japanese business success. In 1981, Ouchi, as well as Pascale and Athos, published books addressing the role of culture in Japanese business success. The following year Deal and Kennedy (1982), as well as Peters and Waterman (1982), published books bringing home to the United States the notion that successful businesses must be concerned with their "cultures."

While anthropologists had been working in business settings for decades and while some work had already appeared in the fledgling field termed "organizational culture" (for example, Baker 1980; Hofstead 1980; Pettigrew 1979), it was the four aforementioned best-sellers that contributed the most toward publicizing and popularizing the culture concept and thus attracted the interest of the business community.

After this initial period of favor in the popular press as the term *corporate culture,* the term *organizational culture* has settled into consulting and academia to describe one more tool to use in studying organizations. In management consulting from the business-training perspective, it is seen as additive, one more piece of the organization. Management interest in anthropology focuses on our methodology as reflected in the several articles published in management journals by anthropologists (Morey and Luthans 1984, 1987; Sanday 1979) and the recent volume published in Sage's Qualitative Research Methods Series by Schwartzman (1993). From the anthropological perspective, organizational culture is holistic, integrated, and superorganic, and embodies some basic theory as well as methodology of our discipline. Under the name of organizational culture it is a young field in anthropology, but in reality it is the continuation of a long heritage of study of complex organizations. Baba's 1986 NAPA bulletin provides a comprehensive account of this history.

The recent research takes several forms. Some of it is found in the study of work (Applebaum 1984); The Society for the Anthropology of Work and its *Anthropology of Work Review* have fostered developments in this area (Sachs 1989). Britan and Cohen, however, set the stage for the development of an anthropology in formal organizations in their article "Toward an Anthropology of Formal Organizations" (1980). Britan (1981) and Dubinskas (1988) have renewed the tradition of industrial ethnography; Dubinskas edited a volume of ethnographies of high-tech corporations. Anthropologists working in the field of international business consulting are describing the anthropological fit (Hamada 1988; Reeves-Ellington 1988; Sherry 1988). David coauthored a text on international business (Terpstra and David 1985). Hamada has conducted extensive research on American and Japanese organizational culture interactions (1991). More work on the dynamics of formal organizations is beginning to appear (Jordan 1990). Baba has studied the development of local knowledge systems among workers (1989). Connors and Romberg have analyzed manager reactions to quality control programs (1991). Other anthropologists, like Briody, are employed by corporations to conduct in-house research, the results of which are appearing in anthropological journals (Briody and Baba 1991; Briody and Chrisman 1991). Others are working in the field of intercultural training (McDougall 1991; Ojile 1986). The *Anthropology of Work Review* published a special issue on organizational culture (Sachs 1989), and several edited collections on organizational culture and cross-cultural management (Hamada and Jordan 1990; Serrie 1986; Sibley and Hamada, in press) are available.

The surge of interest by anthropologists in the 1980s and 1990s is tied to the surge of interest in anthropology by organizational behaviorists. The possibility for cross-fertilization is great (Jordan 1989; Walck and Jordan 1993). Management researchers, however, usually define culture as additive. Culture is one more variable, a characteristic that an organization has. It is usually described as the values and beliefs of an organization but in reality represents the messy human stuff that managers and organizational theorists alike cannot quite figure out what to do with. They do not see culture as the superorganic, the whole that includes all the other variables they study. Morey and Morey's chapter discusses the management mindset regarding organizations. Understanding this mindset is crucial for any anthropologist attempting to enter business consulting.

Organizational Culture Defined and Operationalized: The Advantage of Multiple Theoretical Frameworks in Anthropology

Organizational culture is the study of an organization as if it were a culture, in order to better understand behavior in the organization. The organizational culture approach is the use of the construct "culture" and ethnographic methods to analyze human behavior in complex organizations. While this may appear to be stating the obvious, specific definitions depend on the researcher. In anthropology as a whole, there is no single agreed-upon definition of culture and no single ethnographic technique for uncovering "culture" and, thus, no single anthropological approach. The same is true of organizational culture. All of us working in the field take a slightly different approach and focus on different issues, depending on the problem at hand. For the most part, the work is problem driven. In a practical application such as consulting, the problem to be solved may determine the definition of culture and, in turn, the methodology appropriate for analyzing and solving the problem. For example, one situation might call for a definition similar to Tyler's while another might require one similar to Spradley's. One researcher may concentrate on material artifacts, another on manifested behavior, and another on mental maps.

The cases described in this bulletin illustrate this diversity. Each of the authors defines culture differently and utilizes different methodology. This diversity is a strength. As a consultant, one usually has a particular problem to address. The definition of culture and the methodology it requires may be determined by the problem to be addressed. The cases in this issue present alternatives, and no single approach is necessarily the best for all cases.

There are some unifying threads, however. All the work described here is anthropological, and the reader will recognize definitions, theory, and techniques that she or he has seen used in more traditional contexts. Further, the fact that it is anthropological means the definitions of culture are holistic rather than additive. It also means that, while the researchers may not agree on whether knowledge/norms or behavior or material artifacts should define culture, they all recognize the interplay among these features and the significance they hold as clues to understanding culture. In addition, the authors all see and appreciate the intricacies of subculture and part culture. This allows culture to mean that the organization as a whole may have a culture and also that departments and professional, ethnic, and gender groups can all be viewed as cultures. Organizational culture then becomes a web of interwoven and hierarchical culture groups. In addition, the organization's culture is a part culture in one or more larger cultures that might include regional cultures within one nation, more than one national

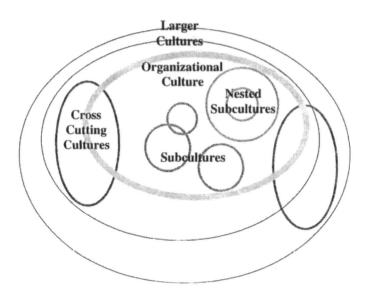

Figure 1. Anthropological perspective.

culture, and even a world culture of international business. The nuances of behavior are made understandable when this diversity is recognized. Figure 1 depicts this view of an organization.

One cannot understand organizations in the modern world without understanding the significance of power. The power dimension is a significant factor in behavior in corporations, at both the organizational and individual level. It is a factor in the behavior of subordinates toward superiors in any office, as well as in the behavior of multinational corporations in the world system. While none of the consultants in this volume specifically address the issue of power, its relevance can be seen in many of the events they describe.

In attempting to understand the organization at hand, each consultant must grapple with identifying the stakeholders. Kogod describes the difficulty that she (as the consultant) had determining which organizational interest was her "client." Making that determination helped her identify the stakeholders in the organization and her own position as a stakeholder among them. Kleinberg points out the problems of organizational loyalty in a binational firm and the confusion organization members sometimes have determining where to place allegiance. Stein describes the grief of organization members at losing their "stake."

Beyond this, the cases represent different approaches to consulting. Each consultant has a different entrée into the consulting field, as well as a unique cultural orientation. The three consultants themselves demonstrate the interplay between personal cultural orientation and research choices. Kogod, for example, owns her own consulting business and is thus herself a manager. Her approach reflects a greater degree of acculturation into the culture of managers than do the approaches of the other two. She has taken advantage of the incredible current interest in managing diversity. She contracts with companies to help them manage diversity, which, she plainly explains, requires changing the organizational culture. Kleinberg is on the faculty of a business school. She is immersed in the culture of management scientists and must broker between that academic culture and her own anthropological one. She has been personally immersed in "foreign" cultures (business-school culture and Japanese culture). She is a specialist in Japanese and American organizational cultures and can explain to companies why there is incompatibility in binational firms and how to change it. Stein's approach is more unique for an anthropologist. He is on the faculty of a university health-sciences center. His focus is on grief. His experiences working with Slovak- and Rusyn-Americans (Ruthenian-Americans), his training at a psychiatric institute, and his work at medical schools contribute to his cultural orientation with regard to the analysis of organizational life. He is acutely aware of feelings of marginality, loss, and mourning, and uses his own emotions as research tools.

Each consultant correlates approach, definition, and method. Kogod's approach is to incorporate management literature, definitions, and techniques in order to talk the language that managers understand. Her definitions are less tied to traditional anthropology and make more use of the organizational literature. Kogod states that culture "includes the systems of values and beliefs that are shaped by life experience, historical tradition, class position, job status, political circumstances, economics, and the work setting. . . . [C]ulture can be investigated, defined, and laid out like a map to a new territory" (p. 27). Culture is "a shared design for living; based on the values and practices of a *society,* a group of people who interact together over time" (p. 30). An organizational culture is then "a learned product of group experience shared over time" (p. 31). When appropriate, she elaborates by using Schein's definition, an indication of the way she has integrated the management material into her anthropological approach.

Kogod conducts a five-day ethnographic inquiry that includes structured interviews, focus groups, collection of critical incidents, and content analysis of past complaints. From this she looks for barriers, those influences that inhibit support for diversity in the workplace. These barriers indicate characteristics of the organizational culture which need changing. In addition, she uses a published psychological test, the Hartman Value Profile, to connect individual behaviors with cultural patterns. Such tests, while not always viewed positively by employees, are understood and accepted by them as a standard management technique.

Kleinberg, on the other hand, takes her model from cognitive anthropology and defines culture as "the acquired knowledge people use to give order to their world, to interpret their experience, and to generate social behavior" (pp. 48–49). She adapts Frake's "cognitive sketch map" to organizations, suggesting that culture in an organization can be understood as the work sketch maps of the employees. She conducted unstructured taped interviews and through a domain analysis of their content discovered nation-specific work sketch maps. Frequently the difficulties in managing both American and Japanese workers in the same company were due to their differing perceptions of "job."

Stein, by contrast, works from psychological anthropology and sees culture as a sense of "we-ness." He sees it in terms of identity and boundaries. Stein's approach is quite useful in an organization undergoing substantial change. He suggests that any fundamental organizational change causes the employees to feel grief. His task is to help people in an organization work through the grief associated with organizational culture change, as changing culture means the "we" in some sense must die. Mourning is the fulcrum of change, and employees cannot accept new structures if they have not mourned and let go of the old. In this day of mergers, downsizing, and plant closings, employees must process their grief over the loss of the old corporate form in order to allow change. Stein's work evokes a positive response from individuals with experience in such situations. Stein uses traditional anthropological methods of participant observation and interviewing from top to bottom in the organization. Far from feigning objectivity, however, he sees himself as the research instrument. He sees his own feelings, his own reaction to the people, as the barometer to understand organizational behavior.

In each case, the author has provided advice and guidelines for appropriate culture change. Kogod develops guidelines (an action plan) for change and conducts training sessions in how to achieve this change. She stresses the importance of feedback and of the role of the consultant as joint problem solver. In Stein's approach the type of change has been determined, and he helps employees adapt to it. Kleinberg uses Huse and Cummings's (1985) structure for organizational change. She directs change in areas of company ideology, work and information distribution, intercultural training, and hiring. Each author has devised techniques for carrying out change that are logical extensions of the type of organizational culture analysis they performed.

No single approach is appropriate for solving every problem. Each approach is "correct" and useful for some problems and not for others. Anthropologists can make use of all these techniques, relying on some more heavily than others, depending on the nature of the task at hand.

The Anthropological Legitimacy of Organizational Culture Work

Organizational culture work raises several concerns that are significant to practitioners and to the entire anthropological community. These are important issues that need to be addressed in this overview of the anthropological approach.

Theoretical Issues: Is This "Culture"?

Many anthropologists consider this work to represent an inappropriate use of the anthropological concept of culture. They argue that the accustomed patterns of behavior and beliefs shared by workers in one company do not constitute "a culture" and that to use the construct in this way is inaccurate and dilutes its value. Such a negative view is in one sense correct. In the traditional anthropological sense, these patterns do not constitute a culture because they do not result from primary enculturation beginning at birth. There is clearly a difference, for example, between the "culture" of the Trobrianders and the "culture" of General Motors. In an organization, the patterns of behavior and beliefs result from secondary enculturation that begins at the time of employment. Training programs, asides from more-seasoned employees, observations regarding rewarded and punished behavior, and a host of other elements contribute to the enculturation that makes an individual a member of the organization's culture. In addition, these employees are members of more traditionally defined cultures resulting from enculturation from birth. If one assumes that an organization has a culture, then it follows that any voluntary association, gender grouping, and a host of other structures have culture. It is difficult to see how one could actually understand cultural behavior if a single individual can belong to so many cultural groups and if culture is so easy to acquire. One could view this as a weakening and misuse of the anthropological construct. On the other hand, one could also view this as evidence of the power of the construct *culture*. My work in organizations convinces me that the culture construct is a valuable and powerful one to apply to human behavior in this setting. It does indeed fill in some gaps and provide some understanding of behavior which other management theories miss. Morey and Morey make this point clearly. Our theory is our strength. Management theory is driven by sociology and psychology and has difficulty bridging the gap between the macro and micro levels of behavior. We have the ability to bridge that gap. We can see patterns. We see ways to understand the behavior of the individuals as part of the pattern of behavior of the whole. While business people are more immediately likely to see the anthropologists' usefulness in understanding foreign cultures, we are equally as valuable to them in understanding their own organization. Our theoretical training is the basis for both.

Furthermore, the term *culture* has meaning in consulting. To satisfy anthropological colleagues who dislike this usage, it would be an easy matter for us to substitute another word for *culture*. Hopefully anthropologists will not do that. The corporate world and the consulting world are very familiar with the term *culture* and are applying it to organizations. If anthropologists want to lay claim to the concept that is rightfully theirs and bring to consulting their useful expertise on the subject, then they had better call the construct by name. To publicize ourselves as anthropologists specializing in organizational culture allows business people to understand, albeit vaguely, what we do. To use a different term or to refuse to perform the work at all would obscure our expertise and give to others (psychologists, sociologists, and other management consultants and organizational behavior experts) one of our specialties.

Theoretical Issues: Is Culture a Meaningful Construct for Describing the Modern World?

My work with organizational culture has led me to see, in a clearer fashion than my previous, more-traditional anthropological work, problems with the anthropological construct *culture*. This construct has been and continues to be central to the field of anthropology. It is one of our claims to difference from the other social sciences. There is some difficulty, however, in applying a construct honed in the study of small, homogeneous, slow-changing societies to the modern world composed of pluralistic, fast-changing societies.

First, *culture* is a fuzzy concept. Not only are there as many definitions of it as there are anthropologists (Gamst and Norbeck 1980; Kroeber and Kluckhohn 1952), but once a definition is stated, identifying culture in a specific human situation is difficult.

Clifford's observations upon watching the trial of the Mashpee Indian land suit point out this problem. At issue in the court case was whether the Mashpee were a tribe and whether they had a distinct "culture." Several anthropologists testified.

> This cornerstone of the anthropological discipline [culture] proved to be vulnerable under cross-examination. Culture appeared to have no essential features. Neither language, religion, land, economics, nor any other key institution or custom was its sine qua non. It seemed to be a contingent mix of elements. At times the concept was purely differential: cultural integrity involved recognized boundaries; it required merely an acceptance by the group and its neighbors of a meaningful difference, a we-they distinction. But what if the difference were accepted at certain times and denied at others? And what if every element in the cultural melange were combined with or borrowed from external sources?
>
> At times the experts seemed to suggest that culture was always acculturating. But then how much historical mix-and-match would be permissible before a certain organic unity were lost? Was the criterion a quantitative one? Or was there a reliable qualitative method for judging a culture's identity? [Clifford 1989:323]

In the pluralistic modern world, almost no anthropological researcher can avoid these questions, even when working with people who have been the subjects of much traditional anthropological research.

In working with American business people, I find myself in a bind similar to the one Clifford describes. I am an anthropologist, and my unique approach to studying business organizations lies in my use of the construct *culture,* but to explain this construct to a nonanthropologist is difficult. Culture is vague and hard to pin down. It is more a shared mindset among anthropologists, a result of the socialization (enculturation) of the training process that is graduate school, than a hard concept. The fact that anthropologists understand it and others do not attests to the "organizational culture" of anthropologists who share a paradigm, a worldview, that is not shared by others and that makes us distinct.

For the way in which I use culture in organizational settings, the comments of Bennett are still apropos. As an anthropologist, I am "an expert on the patterned aspects of group behavior . . . (note we did not say 'culture'!)" (Bennett 1954:171). I am doing "what fieldworkers have always done, building up social wholes ('culture' in the American tradition) through a concentration on significant elements" (Clifford 1989:63).

Such an explanation of culture frequently leads to another point of confusion when discussing the concept with individuals in business. This confusion concerns the difference between Culture and culture, a confusion the Moreys mention in the next chapter. Anthropologists move easily between the notion of Culture, that unique symboling ability of humans and the process it represents, and cultures, the learned and transmitted traditions of unique groups. We mean the first in statements like "culture is that complex whole . . ." and the second in statements like "Dani culture and Trobriand culture exhibit some similarities." Anthropologists tend to move from one usage to the other in the same sentence. Nonanthropologists often miss the shift in level of analysis and are thus even further confused by what we mean by *culture.* Consequently, it is important to explain this distinction as part of an explanation of culture.

Anthropology is entering a new era, and it is time to challenge the traditional construct *culture.* This is not to say the construct should be denigrated but rather to suggest that it be celebrated for its richness. Practitioners can contribute to the further development of its ability to describe the modern world. We can develop models that more adequately describe cultures in which interaction means living and working on a daily basis in a multicultural environment. We can develop models that describe fast-paced change, that identify the act of culture change at the moment it happens. Practice can contribute to theory. New fields in anthropology like intercultural training and management consulting enrich all of anthropology by asking new questions and resurrecting old ones.

Ethical Issues

In the 1980s the community of anthropologists was torn apart by a debate over ethics. At the crux of the argument was the question of whether practicing anthropology was ethical for professional anthropologists. When an anthropologist is hired by a client, be it a government agency or a corporation, to use his or her anthropological expertise to achieve the client's goals with regard to a set of research subjects, many professionals in our community feel there is a dangerous possibility that the rights of the research subjects are in jeopardy. The focus of the debate was the appropriateness of secret research and the rights of research subjects. The ethics debate is complicated and multidimensional (see Appell 1978; Cassell and Jacobs 1987; Fluehr-Lobban 1991). The aspects of it relevant for work on organizational culture are discussed below.

The American Anthropological Assocation's code of ethics should be followed in all anthropological lines of work, and the 1990 Revised Principles of Professional Responsibility permit business consulting work in that it permits proprietary research. Under this code anthropologists still have the ethical obligation to keep informants (employees) from physical, mental, or social harm. This includes specifics like the responsibility not to spy. The AAA code, written for the whole anthropological community, does not consider all of the complicated issues confronting anthropologists in business consulting. The Anthropologists' Ethical Guidelines for Practitioners, developed by NAPA in 1988, further clarify some of the relevant issues. For example, in consulting on organizational culture, one has ethical responsibilities to one's client to carry out the prescribed duties, as well as to the research subjects (who may be the client). One should carefully review any contact and ensure that the rights of all persons affected by the work are secured. Those who hire the anthropologist should be informed up front that she or he intends to protect anonymity of all research subjects.

Certainly, however, there are many ethical dangers in consulting on organizational culture. Some fear that enlightening managers on their organization's culture assists them in manipulating employees. Managers' comments like "How can I use culture as a lever to change behavior?" cause one to suspect that indeed some managers hope that culture will allow them to manipulate employees. The danger of this, however, is not great. Anthropologists are more aware than most that culture represents a complicated process that is just not that easy to direct. Culture is not a behavior pattern that a manager can decree; it is, by definition, something that all employees create and transmit. The long history of applied work in anthropology attests to the difficulty of trying to force people to change their culture. Consequently, while we must be ever aware of protecting the rights of all subjects, culture is difficult to manipulate and does not provide the manager with a secret weapon. Instead, anthropologists as consultants do what all anthropologists do. They listen to and talk with individuals at all levels. By viewing the organization as a culture, we legitimate and value the views and behaviors of the employees at lower levels. Traditional business consulting legitimates the views of managers. Anthropologists, more than other types of business consultants, understand that all members of the organization must be heard for the organization to be understood. We are the consultants who bring the voices of the lower-level employees into the discussion. Doing so should not then allow manipulation because the process of culture change is so complicated.

However, the managers' interest in culture as a tool or lever to change behavior must be seriously addressed. While anthropologists can see the value in studying organizations for the insight such study brings, managers consider insight without action to be a waste of time. They want to see behavior change. They measure the success of a consulting project by the amount of change it brings, not by the amount of insight or understanding it fosters. This difference between the anthropologist's and the manager's definition of success can cause problems. The anthropologist needs to be aware of this potential misunderstanding and confront it in setting out the scope of work, so that all agree on the expectations for the project.

In addition, while culture is not the magic tool some managers perceive it to be, we need to acknowledge the significance of power in the workplace and in capitalist society. We need to recognize that managers are like all humans: some are exploitative. We should guard against allowing our presence or our research to be used to exploit others.

Protecting research subjects does pose a real concern. Even though one ensures their anonymity contractually at the beginning of the project, problems may arise. If one quotes employees, albeit anonymously, in written reports, it is sometimes possible for others to accurately guess the authors of the quotes. The outside researcher who does not know these individuals personally may innocently quote statements that contain phraseology that only one individual in the corporation is known to use and thus unwittingly identify that individual. Or in describing "real" culture, the anthropologist may describe work procedures that are in violation of company policy and cause the company to take actions against a group of workers, even though individual anonymity is maintained (see Graves and Shields 1991 for a more detailed example of this). The individual consultant must constantly be alert to the problems of protecting subjects.

Many of the stickier ethical questions in consulting on organizational culture are ones shared with many areas of applied anthropology. For example, if an anthropologist helps change a job's content, has he or she harmed an employee who cannot adjust? That dilemma is similar to the one faced by an anthropologist who helps change production techniques in rural Guatemala. Has she or he harmed an informant who cannot adjust? If the anthropologist helps raise productivity in the workplace, workers may be displaced. What is the anthropologists ethical responsibility in this case?

There are numerous ethical issues that will surface in working with corporations. (Kogod discusses one such issue in her chapter.) As more of us perform business consulting, more issues will become evident. It is up to the individual anthropologist in consulting or in any line of applied work to be wary of and avoid ethical problems. The fact that there will be ethical issues does not require us to ban this kind of work. It does require us to move into it with caution and to keep the ethical questions always in our minds. As more of us work in business consulting, we may wish to develop a code of ethics specifically for corporate work.

It is not only practicing anthropologists who are wrestling with new ethical issues. The new era in anthropology touches everyone. The old model of colonial-style research is no longer viable. There are few nonliterate populations left who are uninterested in the manner in which their comments are written into published work (Fluehr-Lobban 1991:229). Debates on intellectual property are bringing to the fore the question of ownership of knowledge. Even in traditional areas of anthropological inquiry, the research subjects are raising questions about the ethical nature of protecting their identity while making careers of publishing their ideas. The view of research subjects as passive, powerless, and in need of our protection has given way to one of subjects who are active participants in an interactive research process in which they are involved in the design and outcome of the work. Researchers can no longer hide their work from the subjects nor can they dismiss the subjects' criticisms as a simple reflection of the insider's difficulty in seeing culture clearly. The subjects, whether those be corporate employees or American Indian communities, are holding the researcher accountable for the contents of their reports. This is a new era for all of anthropology and one that we should all welcome.

Conclusion

All of anthropology is entering an exciting new era. Anthropologists have an important contribution to make to the understanding of the pluralistic, fast-paced modern world. Our training and our theoretical base are valuable assets. In the field of business consulting, our understanding of organizational culture fills a void. Our work in organizational culture contributes to both management science and traditional anthropology.

References Cited

Appell, George N.
   1978   Ethical Dilemmas in Anthropology Inquiry: A Case Book. Waltham, MA: Crossroads Press.
Applebaum, Herbert
   1984   Work in Market and Industrial Societies. Albany: State University of New York Press.
Baba, Marietta L.
   1986   Business and Industrial Anthropology: An Overview. NAPA Bulletin, 2. Washington, DC: American Anthropological Association.
   1988   Two Sides to Every Story: An Ethnohistorical Approach to Organizational Partnerships. City and Society 2:71–104.
   1989   Local Knowledge Systems in Advanced Technology Organizations. In Strategic Management in High Technology Firms. Luis Gomez-Mejia and Michael Lawless, eds. Pp. 57–75. Greenwich, CT: JAI Press.
Baker, Edwin L.
   1980   Managing Organizational Culture. Management Review 69:8–13.

Bennett, John
    1954 Interdisciplinary Research and the Concept of Culture. American Anthropologist
        56:169–179.
Briody, Elizabeth K., and Marietta L. Baba
    1991 Explaining Differences in Repatriation Experiences: The Discovery of Coupled and
        Decoupled Systems. American Anthropologist 95:322–344.
Briody, Elizabeth K., and Judith Beeber Chrisman
    1991 Cultural Adaptation on Overseas Assignments. Human Organization 50:264–282.
Britan, Gerald M.
    1981 Bureaucracy and Innovation. Beverly Hills: Sage Publications.
Britan, Gerald M., and Ronald Cohen
    1980 Toward an Anthropology of Formal Organizations. In Hierarchy and Society. Gerald
        M. Britan and Ronald Cohen, eds. Pp. 9–30. Philadelphia: Institute for the Study of Human
        Issues.
Cassell, Joan, and Sue-Ellen Jacobs, eds.
    1987 Handbook on Ethical Issues in Anthropology. Special Publication, 23. Washington,
        DC: American Anthropological Association.
Clifford, James
    1988 The Predicament of Culture: Twentieth Century Ethnography, Literature and Art.
        Cambridge, MA: Harvard University Press.
Connors, Jeanne L., and Thomas A. Romberg
    1991 Middle Management and Quality Control: Strategies for Obstructionism. Human
        Organization 50:61–65.
Deal, Tarrence E., and Allan A. Kennedy
    1982 Corporate Cultures. Reading, MA: Addison-Wesley.
Dubinskas, Frank A.
    1988 Making Time: Ethnographies of High-Technology Organizations. Philadelphia:
        Temple University Press.
Fluehr-Lobban, Carolyn
    1991 Ethics and the Profession of Anthropology: Dialogue for a New Era. Philadelphia:
        University of Pennsylvania Press.
Gamst, Frederick C., and Edward Norbeck
    1980 The Hoghead: An Industrial Ethnology of the Locomotive Engineer. New York: Holt,
        Rinehart and Winston.
Graves, William, and Mark A. Shields
    1991 Rethinking Moral Responsibility in Fieldwork: The Situated Negotiation of Research
        Ethics in Anthropology and Sociology. In Ethics and the Profession of Anthropology.
        Carolyn Fluehr-Lobban, ed. Pp. 130–152. Philadelphia: University of Pennsylvania
        Press.
Hamada, Tomoko
    1988 Working with Japanese: U.S.-Japanese Joint Venture Contract. Practicing Anthro-
        pology: 10(1):6–7.
    1991 American Enterprise in Japan. Albany: State University of New York Press.
Hamada, Tomoko, and Ann T. Jordan
    1990 Cross-Cultural Management and Organizational Culture. Studies in Third World
        Societies, 42. Williamsburg, VA: College of William and Mary.
Hofstead, Geert
    1980 Culture's Consequences: International Differences in Work-Related Values. Beverly
        Hills: Sage.
Huse, Edgar F., and Thomas G. Cummings
    1985 Organization Development and Change. St. Paul, MN: West Publishing.
Jordan, Ann T.
    1989 Organizational Culture: It's Here, But Is It Anthropology? Anthropology of Work
        Review 10(3):2–5.
    1990 Organizational Culture and Culture Change: A Case Study. In Cross-Cultural
        Management and Organizational Culture. Tomoko Hamada and Ann T. Jordan, eds.
        Studies in Third World Societies, 42. Williamsburg, VA: College of William and Mary.

Kroeber, Alfred, and Clyde Kluckhohn
    1952 Culture: A Critical Review of Concepts and Definitions. Harvard University. Papers
        of the Peabody Museum of American Archaeology and Ethnology, 47. Cambridge, MA:
        Harvard University Press.
McDougall, Lorna
    1991 Training as Worldview. Paper presented at the American Anthropological Associa-
        tion 90th Annual Meeting, Chicago, IL.
Morey, Nancy C., and Fred Luthans
    1984 An Emic Perspective and Ethnoscience Methods for Organizational Research.
        Academy of Management Review 9:27–36.
    1987 Anthropology: The Forgotten Behavioral Science in Management History. In Best
        Papers Proceedings of the 47th Annual Meeting of the Academy of Management. Frank
        Hoy, ed. Pp. 128–132. Athens, GA: University of Georgia.
Ojile, Constance S.
    1986 Intercultural Training: An Overview of the Benefits for Business and the Anthropolo-
        gist's Emerging Role. In Anthropology and International Business. Hendrick Serrie, ed.
        Pp. 35–51. Williamsburg, VA: College of William and Mary.
Ouchi, William
    1981 Theory Z. Reading, MA: Addison-Wesley.
Pascale, Richard Tanner, and Anthony G. Athos
    1981 The Art of Japanese Management. New York: Simon and Schuster.
Peters, Thomas J., and Robert H. Waterman
    1982 In Search of Excellence. New York: Warner Books.
Pettigrew, Andrew M.
    1979 On Studying Organizational Cultures. Administrative Science Quarterly 24:570–
        581.
Reeves-Ellington, Richard
    1988 A Manager's Use of Anthropology. Practicing Anthropology 10(1):8–9.
Sachs, Patricia, ed.
    1989 Anthropological Approaches to Organizational Culture. Theme Issue. Anthropology
        of Work Review 10(3).
Sanday, Peggy Reeves
    1979 The Ethnographic Paradigm(s). Administrative Science Quarterly 24:527–538.
Schwartzman, Helen B.
    1993 Ethnography in Organizations. Qualitative Research Methods Series, 27. Newbury
        Park, CA: Sage.
Serrie, Hendrick, ed.
    1986 Anthropology and International Business. Studies in Third World Societies, 28.
        Williamsburg, VA: College of William and Mary.
Sherry, John F.
    1988 Teaching International Business: A View from Anthropology. Anthropology & Edu-
        cation Quarterly 19:396–415.
Sibley, Will E., and Tomoko Hamada, eds.
    In press Anthropological Perspectives on Organizational Culture. Washington, DC: Uni-
        versity Press of America.
Terpstra, Vern, and Kenneth David
    1985 The Cultural Environment of International Business. Cincinnati: Southwestern Pub-
        lishing.
Walck, Christa L., and Ann T. Jordan
    1993 Using Ethnographic Techniques in the Organizational Behavior Classroom. Journal
        of Management Education 17:197–217.

Organizational Culture: The Management Approach

Nancy C. Morey and Robert V. Morey

When about ten years ago we entered the disciplines of management and marketing, we expected that this would merely add new knowledge to our previous base of more than twenty years of anthropological work. We were naive. To shift between fields with such different paradigms is difficult. Management consulting brings one into contact with clients and other consultants who were trained from a very different perspective, even though they are using the concept of organizational culture. They look at things that anthropologists do not think important and ignore those that they consider vital. This view, of course, is reciprocated.

Organizational culture is a concept of interest primarily to management (and less to marketing and other business disciplines); therefore, we are focusing almost exclusively on that field. Coming from anthropology, one is expected to know all about organizational culture. However, what we knew about culture did not have a great deal of relationship to what was expected from us.

The Academic Base from Which Managers Derive Their Orientation

In management consulting, anthropologists encounter clients and other consultants who have been trained in traditional business management. They frequently use the term *organizational culture,* but in a manner quite different from that of anthropologists. The assumptions, methods, and priorities of these individuals are different. They consider data that anthropologists do not, and vice versa.

Management scholars ask different questions in research than do anthropologists, and we believe it important to understand the academic base from which many managers derive their orientations. For example, in general management, researchers are interested in the most effective and efficient ways to attain goals in organizations. This would include information gathered by other specialties within the discipline, specialities like organizational behavior, human resources management, organization development, operations management, and so forth.

In the field of organizational behavior, one of the subfields most concerned with organizational culture, researchers are interested in four dependent variables: productivity, turnover, absenteeism, and job satisfaction. These variables were originally determined largely by the interests of practicing managers. The independent variables that they study to see what influences these dependent variables are of three types: individual-level (biographical characteristics, personality, values, attitudes, ability, perception, learning, motivation, and individual decision making, etc.), group-level (group dynamics, group decision making, leadership styles, power and politics, and intergroup relations and conflict), and organization system-level (organization structure, organization policies and procedures, work stress, national culture, and organization culture).

Organizational behavior and organizational theory are the subfields with which most anthropologists share interests. Organizational theory is at the macrolevel, where most anthropologists operate. This is dominated by sociologists, but anthropological methods *and* theories are relevant in this field.

Organizational behavior (OB) is a young field, only having its current form since the 1960s. Surprisingly, it was actually begun by the anthropologists who initiated the Society for Applied Anthropology and who began its first journal (now *Human Organization*). The original *Journal of Applied Anthropology* was, for many years, the only journal expressly devoted to the study of organizations. Early important names in organizational behavior are also known in anthropology: Eliot Chapple, Conrad Arensberg, F. L. W. Richardson, Leonard Sayles, W. Lloyd Warner, Burleigh Gardner, William Foote Whyte, Melville Dalton, and Donald Roy. Whyte wrote the first textbook in organizational behavior (Whyte 1969; see also Morey and Luthans 1987).

The two fields diverged in the 1960s with the split in management between qualitative and quantitative approaches. Although OB is multidisciplinary (in intent, if not always in practice), it tends to focus on microlevel, psychological approaches to individual behavior, despite an interest in work groups and in the impact of organizational structure on individual behavior. Organizational behavior is the area of academic management which most influences practicing managers concerned about the management of people, and it is the psychological approach with which such managers are most familiar and comfortable.

Anthropologists could contribute most easily to the areas that fall between the cracks. For example, there is relatively little understanding of the impact of organizational structure, or other macrolevel variables, on individual behavior. Those trained in organizational behavior find it difficult to bridge the gap between such micro- and macrolevel phenomena, especially with quantitative techniques.

The anthropologist needs to be aware of this separation between levels of analysis, and to develop a way to explain how our field has always successfully integrated the two. Otherwise, managers could tend to be suspicious of investigators who examine both macro- and microlevel variables. To learn the concerns of researchers in management, the following journals can be consulted: the *Academy of Management Journal* publishes empirical (read: principally statistical) studies, and the *Academy of Man-*

agement Review will also publish conceptual pieces. These are both considered to be top journals. The *Journal of Organizational Behavior and Human Performance* is strongly psychology oriented. *The Administrative Science Quarterly* is very prestigious and oriented toward macrolevel concerns. It is said to be returning to a statistical emphasis after a brief period when it published some works on qualitative research. The *Journal of Applied Psychology* is the principal outside journal in which management scholars publish.

There are also minor journals, such as the *Journal of Management Studies, Human Relations,* the *Journal of Management, Organization Studies,* and a few others. *Organizational Dynamics* and the *Organization Development Journal* publish more practitioner-oriented articles, focusing on work done by people in the subfield of organization development.

How Do Managers Understand Organizational Culture?

The Concept of Culture

In the thinking of most managers, culture is just something else that might be useful to improve the effectiveness and efficiency of organizations, and to help them do their jobs. They want to be told the defining elements of culture in such a way that they can go out and "get it." They want to know what kind of culture will give them what kind of results, how do they acquire it, and whether or not they want it. They become frustrated by not knowing the "best kind of culture" to have.

Managers largely believe that organizational culture can be imposed from the top downward. In addition, most managers think of culture only in terms of the middle and upper levels in an organization. There is little thought given to culture among the operating employees, although this has been changing in recent years.

Management scholars, as opposed to practicing managers, are concerned about where culture fits among the many other variables they want to study. They will become frustrated when not given easily measurable indicators of culture to work into questionnaires for quantitative analysis.

Some managers, especially those with more knowledge of sociology, as opposed to psychology, can begin to understand culture as a holistic concept. However, they have difficulties when anthropologists shift levels of abstraction in using the term. The difference between Culture and culture, which is such a basic shared understanding among anthropologists, has not been grasped in management. Often anthropologists are among the frustrated ones when this distinction is not grasped. We frequently fail to realize that those to whom we are speaking have not followed our shift in levels of analysis. For mutual understanding, it is wise to explain these levels "up front" in a manner that does not sound didactic. However, you should still expect confusion.

Some Useful Aspects of Anthropological Methodology, Theory, and Cross-Culture Expertise

Participant observation. Some people in management, including practicing managers, are interested in anthropological methodology, principally in participant observation. These are, however, relatively few.

The attraction of participant observation is the promise that it holds for getting closer to employees, especially operating employees, and learning what is important to them. Too many upper-level (and even some middle-level) managers feel too isolated from lower levels in their organizations, particularly large organizations. This, as many recognize, is a very good way to never find out the bad news until it is too late. Managers who keep themselves isolated are viewed as unapproachable and not as safe people with whom to share problems.

The 1980s saw a wide popularity of the idea of MBWA (management by walking/wandering around). From the simple act of walking around their firms and speaking to employees on a regular basis, managers learned that they could learn a great deal of important information. They were also able to gain more of the trust of their employees.

Managers, more than management scholars, will frequently recognize the importance of direct contact with people. Where this approach is criticized by managers, it will often be on one of three fronts:

1. First, it lacks reliability for academically trained managers, even when they can be convinced of its validity. However, for consulting it may be useful to remind them that, after all, they are really only interested in this one case. It would be too difficult to explain the merits of the comparative method.

2. Second, it takes too long. Managers are interested in fast results and in knowing immediately for what their money is going. They have to explain expenditures in terms of how they help meet current goals and objectives. The participative approaches of most anthropologists, even when attenuated, often take far too long for managers to be comfortable.

3. Third, and often most important, managers can be understandably nervous about what the anthropologist might learn. They are not certain that they want to allow such an open-ended approach within their firms. Questionnaires can be reviewed and approved, or not approved, but observations and interviews are risky. What will happen with sensitive information? Related to this third problem is the fact that an outsider might not always recognize something as sensitive, or who, within the company, should be allowed to see or hear it.

It is always possible that your research could be restricted and you would not be allowed to use any of it, or that the entire study will be tossed out and not used at all. These are some problems of working with private concerns.

Anthropological theory. Anthropological theory is of very limited interest to management. This is principally because it does not address questions of concern to them. Anthropological theories are much more global than management theories. This is largely because of the heavy dependence upon psychology for the basic approach in management, and as noted above, there are a limited number of issues with which managers are concerned when it comes to managing people. When anthropology does address such issues, the evidence is considered anecdotal because it is not reached through a controlled statistical study.

Managers, as suggested above, are principally concerned with such areas as productivity, absenteeism, turnover, and job satisfaction. In addition, they are interested in motivation, leadership, and practical topics such as how to reduce pilferage. They also may think they want to acquire a particular kind of organizational culture, and want advice on this.

Managers will have to be educated in the fact that an anthropologist can offer much more than this limited range of individual-centered information. It may be wise to work on specific tactics for differentiating anthropology from psychology and also from sociology—especially, in reference to the things that "fall between the cracks" which we mentioned above.

Anthropologists have a strength in knowing how to conceptualize, explain, predict, and modify the impact of structure (formal and informal) on individual behavior beyond the microlevel explanations given by most psychology. Our particular strength is in seeing patterns in individual behavior that become structure (often informal) (see Morey and Luthans 1991). Such patterns generally have to be discovered through participant observation and informed questioning. They are generally not discernible through a questionnaire. This, we believe is a hidden strength of anthropology, the ability to discover patterns in human behavior. It is, after all, these patterns that create all the macrolevel structures. It is also these macrolevel structures that impact on individuals to create additional patterns. The anthropologist can unravel these, both the intended and unintended. Many organization-development specialists (see below) can come close to this skill, but they are not as explicit nor as objective about it as are anthropologists. They attempt to explain their work primarily in microlevel terms.

Some firms may be simply interested in improving general organizational functioning but, of course, in relation to their overall productivity. It may be difficult to explain how particular findings are useful unless you can tie them to concepts such as these. Other firms are accustomed only to "buying" packages of one kind or another, such as specific kinds of training, management development, or orientations for employees going overseas.

There is an area within management, called organization development (OD), which could be the first to find anthropological theory useful. Some managers are familiar with this field and often hire such specialists. There also may be in-house organization-development workers. This subdiscipline has some clear similarities to the field of action anthropology. OD is the study of planned change in organizations. It proceeds, in its practical approaches, in much the same manner as does anthropological fieldwork. Perhaps, for this reason, it is frequently denigrated within management. However, it has its own journals, as noted above *(Organizational Dynamics* and *Organization Development Journal)*, and some of its practitioners are well known and respected.

In marketing, the areas of international marketing, consumer behavior, and advertising are among a few that have benefited to a limited extent from anthropology but could use more input from theory and methodology.

Managers do not comprehend the close relationship between theory and method in anthropology and will not be interested in theoretical explanations for findings, despite recent interest in analyzing companies in terms of models of "primitive" societies. The anthropologist needs to remember, however, that there is a great deal of use to be made of existing theory for understanding many things happening in organizations. It can be useful, for instance, to conceptualize ceremonies as rituals of particular kinds or to see relationships within an organization in terms of dyadic alliances (Morey and Luthans 1991). Clearly, many of the basic understandings we carry about human culture and behavior are as relevant here as they are in Oceania, Africa, or an Amish community.

Cross-cultural expertise. Very few management people are interested in a cross-cultural perspective, in spite of the increasing importance of international business. We can hope that this number will be increasing in the 1990s. The main people in the academic discipline of management doing any kind of cross-cultural research are those born in other countries and speaking other languages. A field called comparative management exists, which might be used to reach managers more easily, but it has little respect.

Geert Hofstede, a Dutch scholar, has chastised management for the implicit assumptions that American management theories have universal application (Hofstede 1980, 1981). It is still too frequent, in spite of the prominence of multinational companies, that the home office (if it is in the United States) lacks interest in understanding the cultures to which it is either attempting to sell or in which it is setting up subsidiaries and/or manufacturing plants. Employees leave unprepared for overseas assignments, and operations overseas are conducted below optimum levels. Such issues will become increasingly vital in the 1990s, because they have such an effect upon productivity.

Other articles in this bulletin will demonstrate the cross-cultural difficulties very well. It is true that studies of Japanese business organizations are popular because of the increasing importance of Japan in the world and that practicing managers are very interested in learning about them. But even such masterful works as Rohlen's 1974 study of a Japanese bank is little known in management, and when it is, the purpose is only to emphasize something exotic, such as the group-oriented aspects of training.

One reason for this may be an habitual lack of historical concern among the majority of managers. Partly because of the intense emphasis on the future (albeit, short-term) in management and the heavy demand for information to see one safely through it, lessons of the past are too often ignored or discounted. After all, how could something written in 1974 possibly have relevance for the 1990s?

Many managers are unaware of the fact that basic cultural changes occur very slowly. They are most aware of rapid technological changes. They do not see that lessons from the human behavior of centuries and even millennia ago can still elucidate organizational behavior today. We can learn about Japan from *The Chrysanthemum and the Sword* (Benedict 1946), as well as from Rohlen's work (1974).

People doing consulting internationally and in multinational firms recognize other kinds of valid and reliable data. They may develop training programs from this, such as the Copeland and Griggs productions *Going International* (1985) and *Valuing Diversity* (a training video).

Books have been written for courses in international business, but relatively little research is being undertaken, and much useful information is certainly not available to the managers who need it. Some books developed are based on good experience, but there are too few of them (Adler 1986; Copeland and Griggs 1985; Phatak 1989; Punnett 1989; Rutenberg 1982).

Managers can attend seminars and workshops and hire consultants, in order to learn about many aspects of the international monetary scene, about legal differences, and about manufacturing issues. However, there are few places to which they can go to gain a broad understanding of culture which they can apply to understand cultural differences in general. Too often the behavioral information they receive deals only in the dos and don'ts of business and social relations in Malawi or Saudi Arabia or Brazil. This would seem to be an area in which anthropology could become extremely useful to practicing managers.

Cross-Cultural Understanding Requires Cultural Understanding

For a real understanding of cross-cultural issues and organizational culture issues, managers need a more sophisticated understanding of culture. The difficulty in communicating anything dealing with culture is that you have to provide so much basic background and explanation before you can make your point. In consulting, an anthropologist must develop as concise and specific an approach as possible. Central assumptions and methods will have to be justified and explained, but not at length, so that you can get on to dealing with more substantive issues. Until there is an accepted body of anthropologists' work on organizations, this will be difficult. A possible interim method might be to fall back on famous names, such as Margaret Mead, to justify your approach. You could also familiarize yourself with the work of anthropologists in organizations (past and present), many of whom discovered the basic notions about organizations that these managers learned in their first courses on the subject (see Morey and Luthans 1987). Today, Andrew Pettigrew is a British anthropologist who is well known in some academic management circles. Leonard Sayles is currently director of the Research Group of the Center for Creative Leadership in Greensboro, North Carolina, a respected research and consulting organization. Some of the work of these individuals could be mentioned and cited.

Collaborators within a firm might be found, in order to help explain your work to others there. An anthropologist could also use a champion for the inevitable times when someone becomes nervous, as they will, because you have begun to know too much.

Ways to Get into Consulting

There are various ways in which you could begin finding work as a consultant. Obviously, to find a firm with a particular problem that you could solve would be ideal. But this may be difficult unless you have cultivated contacts and friendships that will be willing to share this information with you.

Another possibility would be to create for yourself one or more "specialty" areas through which you could begin demonstrating your usefulness and begin making more contacts. Examples might something like "developing cross-cultural sensitivity" or creating a useful training program for managers being sent overseas. Obviously, your choice would depend on the area in which you live and/or want to work. What are the special needs in that area? How do they match your own special strengths?

Anthropologists consulting on organizational culture will have all of the difficulties already mentioned and may encounter new ones of their own. Perhaps the most useful thing they could do for themselves would be to create a succinct, yet accurate, explanation of culture which matches how they intend to work. Create your own definition, modeled after your particular approach. For example, an archaeologist could be quite comfortable with a Leslie White type of definition. An anthropologist working in an organization might be more apt to be thinking about approaches emphasizing meaning, à la Spradley. You may have some other preference. But be ready and able to explain yourself in terms understandable to a layman. Do not forget to make that explanation in terms of the specific benefits you could add to increase the efficiency and effectiveness of the organization or in terms of some similar concern common to management.

Conclusion

We believe that anthropologists can be recognized as extremely beneficial to management, but we also recognize that it will fall upon anthropologists to do the convincing. We know that we have presented a rather negative view, but we must remember that we are anthropologists attempting to convince other people that our knowledge can be useful. Very few of these people are knowledgeable enough to want to seek out anthropologists on their own. They need to be educated.

An important point for anthropological consultants to remember is that you are defeating your purpose if you attempt to compete among yourselves. You need to help each other. Develop professional consulting organizations. Write articles to help each other. Keep in contact. Do not attempt to hide the fact that you are anthropologists by, for example, using a different "cover." You need to plan for the long run, not just this one job. Every anthropologist who succeeds in demonstrating the usefulness of their work to one manager or firm increases the chances for all. They will not merely be spreading their own reputation but that of the field in general.

References Cited

Adler, Nancy J.
   1986   International Dimensions of Organizational Behavior. Boston: Kent Publishing.
Benedict, Ruth
   1946   The Chrysanthemum and the Sword. Boston: Houghton Mifflin.
Copeland, Lennie, and Lewis Griggs
   1985   Going International:How to Make Friends and Deal Effectively in the Global Market-place. New York: New American Library.
Hofstede, Geert
   1980   Culture's Consequences: International Differences in Work Related Values. Beverly Hills: Sage Publications.
   1981   Culture and Organizations. International Studies of Management and Organizations 10(4):15–41.
Morey, Nancy C., and Fred Luthans
   1987   Anthropology: The Forgotten Behavioral Science in Management History. In Best Papers Proceedings of the 47th Annual Meeting of the Academy of Management. Frank Hoy, ed. Pp. 128–132. Athens, GA: University of Georgia.
   1991   The Use of Dyadic Alliances in Informal Organization: An Ethnographic Study. Human Relations 44(6):597–618.
Phatak, Arvind V.
   1989   International Dimensions of Management, 2nd edition. Boston: PWS-Kent Publishing.
Punnett, Betty Jane
   1989   Experiencing International Management. Boston: PWS-Kent Publishing.
Rohlen, T. P.
   1974   For Harmony and Strength: Japanese White Collar Organization in Anthropological Perspective. Berkeley: University of California Press.

Rutenberg, David P.
   1982   Multinational Management. Boston: Little, Brown, and Co.
Whyte, William Foote
   1969   Organizational Behavior: Theory and Application. Homewood, IL: Richard D. Irwin, Inc.

Using Organizational Culture in Consulting: Empirical Examples

The Bridges Process: Enhancing Organizational Cultures to Support Diversity

S. Kanu Kogod

The face of American society in the workplace is rapidly changing in its age mix, gender composition, cultural background, education, and physical challenges. Not only must workers adjust to their work environment, businesses are also learning how to respond to these changes. Previously relied-on human-resources policies and practices, supervisory and management techniques, and interpersonal communications skills are becoming outmoded.

As a result of changing demographic trends and the social, economic, and political forces currently impacting business, now more than ever it is necessary to effectively manage a diverse workforce. I have developed a consulting practice in *managing diversity*. Essentially, our company helps organizations change their organizational cultures to make better use of the talents and contributions of each employee. The concept of organizational culture is essential to managing diversity because diversity is a context issue.

To appropriately manage diversity, the organizational culture must be understood. This includes the systems of values and beliefs that are shaped by life experience, historical tradition, class position, job status, political circumstances, economics, and the work setting. When understood in this manner, culture can be investigated, defined, and presented like a map to a new territory. By identifying these forces and the barriers to change, we are able to address them in terms of planned organizational change.

This article describes an organizational development model using anthropological principles to meet these challenges. The article is addressed to anthropologists who are interested in the issue of managing diversity.

My attempt is to answer the questions: What is *managing diversity?* How can anthropologists address diversity by looking at organizational cultures? What is an anthropological approach to managing diversity? For clarity, I will describe a case example describing a process approach.

While our focus is on American businesses in terms of identifying issues and defining problems, it is likely that similar issues confront other high-technology workplaces in the Western world. My purpose is to demonstrate that understanding and managing human behavior in an organization requires both knowledge of organizational culture and application of anthropological principles to change it. Hopefully, the process described and the case example may be helpful to a broader audience.

The Need for Managing Diversity

In 1987, the Hudson Institute released *Workforce 2000* (Hudson Institute 1987), the now-famous study of the workforce of the future, commissioned by the U.S. Department of Labor. In it, they made predictions about the demographic composition of the U.S. population and workforce until the year 2000.

Among the startling findings were the following projections: Of the 25 million people who will join the workplace between 1985 and 2000, 85 percent will be minorities and women. White males will account for only 15 percent of the net additions to the labor force; the remainder will be comprised of white females, and immigrants and minorities (of both genders) of various black, Hispanic, and Asian origins. The Hispanic and Asian populations will each grow by 48 percent, the black population will grow by 28 percent, and the white population will grow by only 5.6 percent. In fact, it is projected that sometime in the next century, non-Hispanic whites will no longer retain their majority status in the United States.

This dramatic shift in the demographic makeup of the population and the workforce has enormous implications for American employers, who have traditionally relied on white males to fill the majority of their positions. The growing number of women, older workers, foreign-born workers, and physically challenged employees have a profound impact on an organization's needs, styles, expectations, and social policies.

Employers know that they will be competing for increasingly scarce talent, of whatever gender, age, race, or ethnicity, and that they want to be able to retain those workers once they have brought them on board. High turnover is a costly and bothersome phenomenon. It therefore behooves them to do what they can to make the workplace a tolerable, if not supportive and satisfying, environment in which culturally diverse individuals (along with those of different ages and sexes) can work together effectively, productively, and—one would hope—comfortably. The following statements illustrate the emerging attitude within the business community about why there is a need to manage diversity.

- It will help "transform fear and ignorance of foreigners into comprehension and cooperative skills."

- "If you start now and build a climate in which all groups feel comfortable, you enhance your recruiting possibilities and your ability to attract talent."
- "Countless hazards are created by communication problems, cultural differences in motivational and value systems, diverse codes of conduct, even differences in orientation to fundamentals such as perception of time and space."
- "Competition requires full utilization of all our resources. If we develop only white males, we're not really developing our resources, and that is a complete waste."

Gradually in the early 1990s, the process of valuing diversity is seen less and less as an avenue for fulfilling affirmative action and legal requirements. On the contrary, valuing diversity is a positive, voluntary, pro-business activity, as opposed to belonging to the legal and regulatory environment in which many equal employment opportunity (EEO) and affirmative action (AA) programs exist. There is a *pull* to fulfilling organizational potential rather than a *push* to comply with requirements.

In the past several years, large businesses have become increasingly savvy about interpreting the diversity issue to a broader audience—one that is more interested in the bottom line. Organizations such as Motorola, Hughes Aircraft, and Northern States Power Company (NSPC) tie diversity to overall business aims.

Anthropological Principles at Work

An anthropological definition for managing diversity (adapted from Thomas 1991:26) that we use is that *managing diversity* means "to enhance processes and implement practices that continually move the organizational culture closer to welcoming multiple perspectives by tapping into the talents and contributions of all employees."

Diversity is a context issue. To capitalize on diversity, the organizational culture must be understood, especially the variety of values and assumptions held by dissimilar people in an organization. Once the variety of values are examined, a set of core shared values can be communicated. The core values help define the culture change. Keep in mind that the result we are after is to create a process that continually moves the organizational culture closer to welcoming multiple perspectives and tapping into the talents and contributions of all employees.

Involving diverse employees in decision making is a primary means for welcoming their contributions. This means managers can no longer issue autocratic demands and expect those at lower levels to carry them out without question. Managers are accountable but not by closely held control. Instead, managers need a process by which they can motivate, coach, direct, plan, organize, and lead diverse employees to effectively and efficiently meet their organization's business aims.

Multiple perspectives are encouraged, while still honoring and pursuing the fundamental financial needs of the organization. We must recognize that, in organizations, today's immediate needs may be unimportant tomorrow. Management consultants must be able to facilitate a process approach to changing corporate cultures which will be embraced by those in the organization so that they continue to employ practices that lead them closer to their aims.

As suggested above, there are several layers to addressing diversity, and we must attend to all of them for a long-term change effort to work:

1. Acceptance of one's own identity (and areas of internalized oppression);

2. Ability to be flexible and accommodating to those who are different from oneself in terms of language, culture, and physical appearance;

3. Power and capability to change the current culture and establish an organizational mission that will support diversity goals;

4. Capacity for implementing strategies that involve employees in the culture change process.

Organizations that offer training alone address the first two layers of diversity. The second two layers address the overall organization. These are the areas of culture change that we seek to address.

As anthropologists, we have long recognized that culture is not suddenly created, nor is it easily changed. Culture is the (permeable) boundary that limits infinite possibilities (Joe Duffy, personal communication, November 1992). When working with client organizations, the definition of *culture* that we use is "a shared design for living; based on the values and practices of a *society,* a group of people who interact together over time. People imbibe culture through the early process of socialization in the family, and then this process carries over to the ways people perceive themselves and the world."

We explain the importance of understanding culture in the following manner: Because we learn to perceive our world through our cultural glasses, it becomes essential to get as clear a prescription as possible. When we uncover our shared mental models (Senge 1990:174–204) along with those that differ from our own, we are in a much better position to *anticipate* and *interpret* events that we experience from a culturally relative point-of-view.

The attitude we promote to clients on the interpersonal level is *cultural relativism,* the attempt to understand another's beliefs and behaviors in terms of that person's culture. While each individual in the organization is different and each presents a unique perspective, what is shared is the organization. That includes understanding an organizational culture in terms of its values, traditions, rituals, myths, and so forth.

An *organizational culture* is a learned product of group experience shared over time. When appropriate, we use Schein's definition of *organizational culture:*

> a pattern of basic assumptions—invented, discovered, or developed by a given group as it learns to cope with its problems of external adaptation and internal integration—that has worked well enough to be considered valid and therefore, to be taught to new members as the correct way to perceive, think, and feel in relation to those problems. [1991:9]

While it exists within a larger host culture, an organizational culture can, nevertheless, strongly shape one's *worldview*—a simplified model of the world that helps us make sense out of all we see, hear, and do.

In our training workshops, we define *worldview* and *values:* How do we know if our view of the world makes sense? When our worldview is in line with our society's values and our ability to anticipate and interpret events we experience. Values are the standards we use to determine if something is right or wrong, okay to do. Often values are the unexamined assumptions, never fully articulated, that guide our actions. Values vary from organization to organization and, even more so, from culture to culture.

Again, usually these ideas are implicit; they range from seemingly inconsequential rules for anything from when to hand out a business card to who sits with whom at lunch. In particular, power relationships, work habits, and language special to the organization are examined for their impact on managing diversity. Just as these rules provide guidelines for appropriate behavior, they also color our interpretation of the behavior of others. When our clients understand that these "implicit" cultural assumptions either inhibit or promote expressions of diversity, they, too, become fascinated with the dynamics of culture. They want to understand their own organizational culture better.

An anthropological approach to managing diversity emphasizes that each organization must clarify for itself and consolidate values that guide the performance of those who work together. Understanding the dynamics of culture provides a useful framework for interaction no matter to which cultural group others belong. Studying organizational culture today is especially interesting to practicing anthropologists because it is an open system in constant interaction with many expanding environments and is composed of a multiplicity of groups, with a variety of interests and skills (frequently at cross-purposes), arranged in hierarchies and associated in networks with anywhere-from-weak-to-strong ties.

The ideal result of applying anthropological principles to managing diversity? Ongoing support for creating an organizational culture that develops systems that support the talents and contributions of all employees. When management and employees seek and choose the practices and goals that will enhance characteristics of the work setting, achieving results makes the fruit of success that much sweeter—and that much more viable.

Table 1. The Bridges Process (SM): A 12-Step Approach.
Used by permission of Bridges in Organization, Inc.

---

1. Analyze current reality and define the issues.
2. Create a clear and widely agreed upon vision of future reality.
3. Identify the stakeholders who must be involved in the planning and implementation process.
4. Distinguish what prevents realization of the vision by comparing the current situation to the ideal situation.
5. Conduct a *Barriers Analysis,* an integration of challenges to the organization's vision. It includes specific constraints in organizational structure, operations, and human resources which are contrary to supporting diversity.
6. Create a whole picture of the people involved, tasks to consider, and systems for implementing change.
7. Assess potential impact on the whole organization if all these strategies are set in motion.
8. Develop an action plan for agreed-upon management strategies and training implementation.
9. Implement management strategies and training.
10. Monitor and refine the training and the new strategies by eliciting perceptions of all those involved.
11. Evaluate the training process by analyzing the pre- and postassessments.
12. Provide feedback on utility and effectiveness of new management strategies in a written report of the findings presented to top management.

The Process We Use

In order to build multicultural bridges at work, a broad framework for identifying behavioral and social processes must be provided—the holistic approach. Both information about a particular ethnic group or factor, and also generalizable guides to meet any and all situations, are used in the culture-sensitive approach to improving performance in the workplace. Teamwork is stressed in communications, goal-setting, meetings, and coordination within the team. Aids and guides such as the feedback review can be used in clarifying the relationship of cultural values to performance objectives.

We have applied the principles of anthropology in a framework for guiding organizational culture change (see Table 1). This 12-step process provides direction for introducing the valuing and managing of diversity in large organizations. Like the approach of other management consultants, it is used to promote the new paradigm of diversity—to value all differences and welcome multiple perspectives.

Currently in corporate America, the most-sought-after remedy for addressing diversity is training managers and implementing awareness workshops for employees. For our clients, we promote focusing on the process that will make training meaningful and carry over to real change in the workplace. The process captures the standard method for developing training:

- analysis
- design
- development
- implementation
- evaluation.

It also goes beyond to provide feedback systems, management strategies, and new resources to support organizational transformation. The uniqueness of this process is the focus on both the organization and individual employees in a two-way exchange that is supported by the system. Many people have opportunities to provide meaningful contributions.

The aim of a process approach is to meet the challenges of cultural diversity and its influences on behavior both internal and external to the organization over time. Merely training to elicit overt behavior—politeness and sensitivity—will not accomplish support for the valuing of diversity on an ongoing basis.

In order to support an organizational culture that will attract and retain service-oriented staff and management, there must be a clear, inspiring, and widely agreed upon "vision." The organizational setting should be characterized as genuinely caring about the professional growth and development of each person.

What we are after is a process approach, one that values the end results but also recognizes that any reformation of policies and practices must be coherent with the actual day-to-day practices. A process approach is based on an anthropological view of organizations. It takes into account the considerable time and thought it takes to introduce this type of change in an organization.

Feedback systems are linked through the manager's active involvement in the change process. (Managers are not just told and then expected to carry out orders; likewise, they are not just judged and then expected to listen to the judgment.) Management effectiveness relies on the skill and attitudes of individual managers, as well as the capacity of the organization to support them. Feedback and rewards for good performance help to shape the desired environment. Good performance for all encourages innovation, self-development, and leadership abilities.

Our process has 12 steps that make it possible to be consistently aware of a particular organizational culture. It emphasizes the problem-solving capability of the system by encouraging a series of steps in introducing the value of diversity. Without placing the vision of diversity into its context, pursuit of valuing diversity can do more harm than good since it raises employee expectations without much hope of being sustained.

Case Example: Green & Black, Inc.

The following example illustrates how the process is applied and how anthropological principles help to guide it. While there are many interesting aspects of the project, our discussion will be limited to relevant issues directly pertaining to anthropological principles. A fictitious company name is used; also other minor descriptors are changed to protect the identity of the client.

Green & Black, Inc., is a small business specializing in providing scientific and other professional services to larger companies. The company was founded by two white males, with scientific expertise in their related fields.

In the past 12 years, Green & Black grew from a small, collegial team to a total staff of over one hundred employees with several project teams and five principal lines of business. As the company grew, it became increasingly difficult to become more than superficially acquainted with newcomers, particularly outside one's team. The atmosphere of the workplace changed, and it became necessary to manage. The company has been moving from an entrepreneurial operation to one that is professionally managed.

While white males own the company, three women sit on the 12-member executive committee. About 25 percent of the total census is comprised of African Americans, Filipino Americans, and other Asian American groups mostly in scientific areas and administrative support. Ages are concentrated between young employees in their twenties and those between 40 and 50 years old. About half the company is female.

Green & Black, Inc., prides itself on the organization's overall cooperation, but some recent newcomers have had a more difficult time "fitting in." Complaints about subtle discrimination began to surface. Perceptions of "bending over backward to please those who are culturally different" raised concerns about reverse discrimination.

The staff providing direct services was composed of myself, a white female, and two African American management consultants, Rick and Katy. We were initially hired to address the diversity issue by "adopting policies and practices that support the value of diversity in the workplace . . . to introduce various strategies (particularly training) to support the value of diversity in all levels of the firm—from the owners to senior associates to the professional and administrative staff" (from proposal to Green & Black, September 1990, by Bridges in Organizations, Inc.).

Our approach was explained to the client from the outset and was a selling point as far as they were concerned. At our initial introduction, we emphasized a "valuing differences" approach based on changing the culture to support the people in it. We explained that we do not see diversity as a problem but rather a learning opportunity and that this process would be a "learning process." We went on to say that we have no recipe for success and that we cannot even point to another organization as a role model for having attained all their diversity goals. "Nevertheless," we said, "the process we use will guide you to realizing the vision you set for yourselves."

As emphasized above, the client follows the steps in The Bridges Process (SM). While step one (current reality), step five (barrier analysis), step seven (impact), and step twelve (findings and written report) are the primary responsibilities of the consultants, the client has the option of proceeding independently. At any time during the process, other sessions are scheduled upon request. Telephone support is available throughout the duration of the project.

At the initial meeting, we addressed a diversity committee and explained our process to them. In the session, we went over each step in our guideline including the major outputs: developing management strategies and training to support diversity. We explained that the process involves people from all levels in the organization. Nonetheless, for change to be both positive and acceptable, the process must begin at the top. The list below describes our initial deliverable services and projects that support various steps in The Bridges Process (SM). The list outlines the primary responsibilities of Bridges in Organizations, Inc.

- Provide *executive briefing* sessions to provide information and guidelines to top management, which allows the leadership to clarify their current reality, future goals, and the disparity between the two.
- Conduct five days of *ethnographic inquiry:* structured interviews, focus groups, collection of critical incidents, and content analysis of past complaints. The purpose of the *ethnographic inquiry* is to collect data about perceptions, complaints, values, and implicit influences affecting the organization. This data is used in the *barriers analysis.* Management strategies and training objectives are all influenced by the results of the data-analysis phase.
- Complete a systematic *barriers analysis,* in order to create a succinct listing of specific internal and external influences that inhibit support for diversity in the workplace. When critically examining problems, it is often easy to jump to solutions. The analysis helps to determine how the issues are connected and the impact of change before introducing the change.
- Offer individual management assessments of the leadership using the *Hartman Value Profile* (see Appendixes 1 and 2). The profile identifies specific strengths and weaknesses of an individual; interpretive feedback targets areas considered important to success in a given organization.
  Unlike any other assessment instrument, the Hartman Value Profile (HVP) describes the way a person thinks. It is based on the research of Robert S. Hartman, the founder of modern axiology, the science of values. Hartman constructed a method for measuring value concepts which allows us to relate potential biases, values, and the clarity of one's perceptions of themselves and the world around them. Essentially, the HVP describes mental models.

- Present findings of *barriers analysis* and *big picture* (where we are so far) to top management in a management retreat. Establish *benchmarks,* outputs that demonstrate the organization's movement closer to realization of the vision.
- Continue to guide the process as deemed necessary by project staff. The project coordinator plays multiple roles according to the task. The roles are:
  — objective observer
  — fact finder
  — process counselor
  — joint problem solver
  — culture broker
  — trainer
  — informational expert
  One of the roles of the consultant is to act as a joint problem solver. By offering alternatives and participating in decisions related to action plans, we ensure success of the project. However, the level of consultant activity in this role is determined by the client.
- Conduct three one-day training sessions, "Cultural Encounters in the Workplace," for all staff. Elicit *action plans* from each participant. These plans allow participants to commit to one action that they can personally accomplish according to their interest and level in the organization.
- Prepare a *participant's manual* to guide the training sessions. The manual includes worksheets for supporting the workshop activities, readings for understanding diversity, and resources for gaining more information.
- Assess potential impact on the whole organization if all the strategies proposed by management and in training sessions are set in motion. Include *potential impact of changes* in final report.
  Action plans that were developed by the project staff and in the management retreat are combined with the action plans submitted by participants in the training. Once again, if all the suggested actions were implemented, what would be the *impact* on the organization? Specific strategies are endorsed.
- Present a written report to top management on effectiveness of new management strategies.

Once the project was underway, it became apparent that people, especially top managers, were confused about the focus of the project and the definition of diversity. Did this mean the company wanted to adopt new AA/EEO promotion and recruitment policies? Did it mean prejudice-reduction training? Was the aim to provide touchy-feely training so everyone got along better?

The project was renamed the Corporate Culture Management Project (CCMP—the company loves acronyms) so that the emphasis would remain on the culture itself and the activities we proposed would make sense to the organization.

We began the project with several sessions of the company's executive committee. The outcome was the development of the following *vision* to inspire the desired goals for Green & Black:

> Green & Black is a business committed to quality where everyone is motivated to serve our customers. People from different backgrounds with different personal values are appreciated and rewarded for contributing to the company's success. We work together in an environment of creativity, openness, trust and respect.

To describe *current reality,* we conducted an ethnographic study: structured management interviews, focus groups, analysis of critical incidents, and observation. In general, the *barriers analysis* is developed from the findings of the current-reality description, in comparison with themes derived from the vision. The barriers analysis represents an integration of challenges to supporting diversity at Green & Black. The *barriers* are gleaned from the management's findings, the focus group's findings, and the consultant's observations. In this case, the barriers were then categorized according to the four related themes derived from the vision statement:

- Quality, motivation, and service;
- Diversity, rewards, and recognition;
- Teambuilding;
- Climate setting, work environment, and corporate climate.

Here is a sample of barriers related to the theme of "quality, motivation, and service":

- Not enabling others to act on their own stifles innovation and creativity; both staff and managers need to be both held accountable for their own mistakes and also recognized for their extraordinary efforts. People have expressed intense desire for credit for their work and acknowledgment for their contribution to the organization.
- While many people enjoy working with their colleagues on specific projects, people (in general) do not express a strong sense of loyalty or stake in the success of the whole company.

Here is a sample of barriers related to the theme of "diversity, rewards, and recognition":

- Diversity is of interest to many, but they are not sure what it means to them and to Green & Black. Of greater concern are those who deny differences, with statements like "Everyone is the same to me but some I like more than others," or "I don't care what somebody is. I treat everyone the same." These statements reflect a lack of exposure to diversity and greater comfort with people who are similar to oneself.

- Several well-meaning people express like and respect for individuals who are different, but they seem to be surprised by competence. Others feel diversity means that quality standards will be compromised. These perceptions are a detriment to valuing diversity.
- There is a lack of awareness of gender issues. "Lack of fit" at Green & Black is often due to an inability to adapt to a predominantly male style of speech. Male styles tend to be direct; listening is neutral, and small talk includes banter and one-liners. Women tend to listen with affirmation and to seek connections. Women who get ahead at Green & Black adopt male listening and speech styles. The men who are better liked (including one well-noted leader) are more responsive to female styles of speech.

The barriers analysis also included *positive findings supportive of diversity.* Below are several examples:

- Green & Black is profitable.
- People at all levels are aware of the opportunities for growth and economic success.
- Green & Black's image and reputation in the community and with clients is positive.
- The level of talent, technical skill, and expertise amassed at Green & Black is top-notch.

It was these activities—data collection, analysis of current reality, and presentation of the findings—that utilize the special talents of the anthropologist studying organizational cultures. These are the areas of special contributions to our clients. But anthropology also helps us to conduct ourselves as management consultants.

Anthropologist as Management Consultant

While I have had a great deal of experience working with organizations, this project contained new elements that were of great challenge to me. For one, most of my other work had been with government, social-service, and nonprofit agencies. Other projects for larger corporate organizations were clearly defined up front. This was one of the first projects that allowed me to be an "anthropologist." The principles described above helped me to determine how to make decisions about the project—especially in terms of its challenges.

One of the first obstacles I hit as project coordinator was timing. The start of the project was delayed for two months due to travel schedules and other business priorities. By insisting on commitment up front, we had to assure that all 12 executive-committee members would attend the executive briefings. Scheduling activities and rescheduling activities continued to be a timing problem throughout the project, and so the project schedule was continually being modified.

The *principle of timing* states that planning for change must follow the rhythmic pattern of the group. Thus, it was up to me to be flexible and accommodating. While that sounds good, in reality its difficult to practice when *time* is basically what management consultants are selling. To resolve the issue early on, we came to an agreement that any rescheduling of appointments or activities needed to take place 48 hours before an event; otherwise the time would be billed.

Next came my struggle with defining the identity of my client. Was my client the managing partner (Tom)? the owners? the executive committee? or the organization as a whole? Having sworn fealty years ago to the "powerless" in a group, my struggle was intensified by the fact that, without Tom's authority, there would be no project at all. On the other hand, I felt that I could be a spokesperson and perhaps an advocate for changes that many people expressed to me as needed. Many of these changes in policy fell well beyond the scope of the project, but my first inclination was to help on all counts.

The client-identity question almost stymied the whole project after several head bashings with Tom over the scope of the project. In plain jargon, this was his baby, and he wanted to call the shots. He wanted to keep it limited to the objectives originally described; I wanted to add on other activities that would enhance the overall success of the project. The essence of the struggle is reflected in a memo (an oxymoron, since it turned out to be 12 pages long) that I sent to the two owners. The following is an excerpt from this memo:

MEMORANDUM

SUBJECT: Corporate Culture Management Project

The activities and events shared so far in this project have maintained high quality standards and warm interpersonal communications—the values that are so important to Green & Black and Bridges. This has made the project exceptionally rewarding for Rick, Katy, and me. . . .

In order to achieve success with the project and support you in meeting your management challenges, we would like to meet with you to explore the interrelationship between the project and your current management needs. You can, if you choose, do this as part and parcel of the CCM Project and The Bridges Process.

To be more specific, Rick, Katy, and I recognize the relationship between the mission of the Corporate Culture Management Project and the challenge you now face as you redefine the management culture of your firm. Certain themes and assumptions (most of which you are aware) continue to be issues in the firm, and these themes are cross-purposes for the results we hope to achieve. Although we continue to reaffirm your ownership of the process and we don't intend to resolve all the issues at this time, we are aware [that], in order to achieve success in the project, we must identify the assumptions and plan for change. . . . [*Themes and assumptions were listed.*]

INPUTS

Factors working in our favor are:
• Strategic planning—as the need for employee satisfaction has become a goal, so [has] the understanding that satisfied employees help us achieve our business objectives.
• The possibility that managing diversity will promote the ability to compete in the international market as well as teach consultants to value marketing and sales in the 1990s.
• The recognized need to support the move from being an entrepreneurial organization to being an organization of professional managers.

Factors working against our favor are:
• The narrow focus of the CCM Project as currently defined. A single-focus program that primarily targets interpersonal relations without getting at real business objectives will have a transitory effect on the overall organization.
• The lack of role clarity and expectations between the consultants and the Green & Black client. Is our client Green & Black, and within that is our client the chief operating officer, the owners, or the 12 top managers?

To collaborate means to discuss how the stages of consultation will be carried out, on all aspects of the problem.
Areas of collaboration include: planning how to inform the organization of the project, deciding who is involved at what stages, generating the right kind of data, interpreting the results of the diagnosis, deciding how to make a change.
Our assumption is that our specialized knowledge, along with management's understanding of the organization, allows for joint problem solving. Joint attention is given to technical information and human interactions. Communication is two-way. Implementation responsibilities are determined by discussion and agreement.

The question of client identity was finally answered—Tom, the managing partner, was my client. As a result of the memo, our various roles were clarified. Thus, I came to clearly respect Tom's control and the *principle of authority* and how power affects incorporation of change into the system. Again, without his sanction, there would be no project. On the other hand, as a result of my clarity in the memo about our roles, Tom finally accepted me as a collaborator.

Furthermore, the memo proved to be of great benefit in other ways. It went on to state various suggestions for enhancing the project. Tom and the other top managers who read it were very impressed with the depth of perception and knowledge of the company's real issues. Some felt it was a marketing piece; others felt that it communicated issues too close to home and should be stashed away.

The primary outcome was much greater trust, commitment, and understanding between Green & Black and Bridges. The *principle of feed-*

back states that the system is continuously recharged by feedback on what the system has done.

Another early challenge was the Hartman Value Profile. The assessment piece brought up skepticism and vulnerability for the executive-committee leadership: how could this task give them any meaningful information and what was the purpose of looking at their management potential? The resistance was expressed by not returning the forms on time, not properly completing them, and so on.

In spite of this resistance, I kept on selling the assessment to the recipients. Finally, each person had an individual feedback session. Insight gained by such a tool incorporates the *principle of worldview*. To successfully incorporate a new element in a organizational culture, it is necessary that it also become part of the worldview. By showing them that I had an understanding of their *mental models*, I was able to have an influence on their actions.

When the group composite HVP was presented, we had our first success at team building. People began to really understand what we meant by "welcoming multiple perspectives." The *principle of initial success* was applied to an almost easily achieved goal. This initial success in terms of the overall project, however, was very important in paving the way to commitment for future events in the project.

Conclusion

All things considered, being an anthropologist in corporate America is not easy (Zemke 1989). We have a strong, early affiliation with our academic peers, and we have our own mental models of the ecstacy of studying native cultures in long, extended fieldwork settings. Consequently, we have to shift our awareness in the way we view our contributions, and we have to perform a major transfer of skills to all kinds of settings—some of which we may have strong biases about. For me, meeting this challenge has been both personally and professionally rewarding. Currently in corporate America, diversity is at the forefront of organizational issues. Many larger organizations are going beyond awareness training to hiring in-house "diversity" professionals. While many have strong management skills and familiarity with the issues of diversity, few of these professionals have a cohesive plan for facilitating organizational-culture change that ties into their strategic plan and/or other organizational initiative such as total quality management (TQM). Both diversity and quality initiatives advocate organizational-culture change to be successful. In-house diversity professionals need guidance (especially from anthropologists) to link these as organizational development processes.

We, as anthropologists, are able to apply our holistic, analytical techniques to describing the themes and compelling forces that support or diminish the welcoming of multiple perspectives. This can be a great boon to corporate leaders who are truly willing to embrace the changes bringing us closer to the 21st century.

References Cited

Hudson Institute
 1987 Workforce 2000: Work and Workers for the Twenty-first Century. Indianapolis: Hudson Institute.
Schein, Edgar
 1991 Organizational Culture and Leadership. San Francisco: Jossey-Bass.
Senge, Peter M.
 1990 The Fifth Discipline: The Art and Practice of the Learning Organization. New York: Doubleday.
Thomas, Roosevelt
 1991 Beyond Race and Gender. New York: AMACOM.
Zemke, Ron
 1989 Anthropologists in the Corporate Jungle. Training 26(4):48–54.

Appendix 1

Used by permission of Bridges in Organizations, Inc.

BRIDGES
IN ORGANIZATIONS
INCORPORATED

THE HARTMAN VALUE PROFILE SYSTEM:
**An Assessment Instrument
for Managing Diversity**

What is the Hartman Value Profile?

The Hartman Value Profile (HVP) System is derived from the research of Robert Hartman. He developed a way to measure the clarity, balance and bias of our thinking based on the *structure* of our personal value system. Two critical aspects of diversity are measured by the HVP. First, it identifies those characteristics that make a person unique and second, how one sees themselves in terms of their world.

Each person views the world in his or her own unique way-- even when cultural patterns are similar, each person has a distinctive view. Views of the world are based on an infinite number of factors that make up a person's experience from the time they are born until the time they die. It is this individual structural perspective that influences one's decisions, determines one's actions, and what is attended to or ignored. In other words, we cannot change behavior until we clearly understand the underlying structures holding it in place.

Why an assessment before training?

The Values Profiles provide a report of where a person is now. It is a point-in-time picture of a person's capacities which can and will change over time. The reports provide feedback on the way a person perceives themselves and the world. The "inner world" of self and the "outer world" of others is described on three levels of value.

This report is used to help people understand themselves, their contributions to their working group and the cultural context which contributes to effective organizations. The *Group Report* provides an audit of group strengths and weaknesses so that all these factors can be addressed in a training program.

How do the profiles deal with cultural differences?

Through value analysis, each person's unique patterns can be described and then compared to other's in the group. In this computerized analysis, patterns emerge which demonstrate how clearly they make decisions or judgements in three dimensions (personal, interpersonal and systemic), what people are paying attention to, and the balance between themselves and the world. Armed with this information about individuals and the group, consultants can choose from creative options for communicating, relating, problem-solving and for planning personnel resources. For training, learning objectives can focus on enhanced personal mastery, teamwork, quality, leadership, etc.

BRIDGES
IN ORGANIZATIONS
INCORPORATED

Three Dimensions in Two Worlds

	World	Self
Intrinsic: Unique	Empathy	Self Esteem Fulfillment
Extrinsic: Functional	Practical Thinking	Role Awareness Enjoyment
Systemic: Structural	System Judgement	Self Direction Meaning

How does the HVP benefit organizations?

Specific reports can be generated from the overall profiles which then help a person see the effects of one's own biases, positive-building values and attitudes, negative-blocking values and attitudes, and overall tendencies on a number of measures related to management, sales, service or development.

What is the process for collecting and distributing the data?

Interview Phase
Application of the Profile to each person.

Data Analysis
Evaluation-- a computerized analysis of each individual and a composite profile of the group.

Data Feedback
Individual and confidential feedback sessions to report on the findings. Opportunity to coach that person regarding the meaning of focus, clarity and balance issues for one's life and to develop effective strategies for personal and professional growth.

Setting Workshop Objectives
Objectives for group feedback sessions are derived from the group analysis and composite data. Problem-solving strategies are applied to the real needs of the group.

Group Feedback
Composite profile of the group is presented in a workshop setting so that the group can pinpoint and value differences in the group. Opportunity to focus on specific group needs such as celebrating strengths, examining potential communication blocks, enhancing teamwork, etc.

Executive Report
A report of the findings of the composite profiles and the results of the workshop session is given to top management.

Appendix 2

DIRECTIONS

Each of the following assessments consist of 18 unique words or phrases.

Each represents something upon which individuals place different value. Value in this case means what you consider to be the best or what you consider to be the worst --- either **good or bad.**

The profiles should be completed in consecutive order. To properly score each instrument, please read each of the 18 items.

1. Write the number 1 in the box by the word or phrase that you feel is **best** --- that you value the **most.**

2. Write the number 2 in the box by the word or phrase that you feel is **second best** — the next most **valuable.**

3. **Then continue numbering items that you consider the next most valueable — until you've numbered them 1 through 18.** The least valuable or worst item should be number 18.

4. After filling in all the boxes, you might want to go back and review your responses, then enter your final responses.

REMEMBER:

Number 1 will be the word or phrase that's **most valuable** to you; 18 will be the **least** valuable to you.

Only use the numbers 1 through 18. Only use each number one time.

Decide quickly how you feel about each item. Don't overly dwell on each ranking. Your initial feelings or thoughts are probably the most accurate ones.

Name _____

Social Security No. _____ Date _____

Company Name _____

THE HARTMAN VALUE PROFILE (ONE)

Practice | | Final

1 Profile A:
By Robert S. Hartman, Ph.D.

NAME

COMPANY

After you have finished, please
check to make sure that you have
used all the numbers from 1
through 18, without repeating any.
(Start with your number 1 and find
each number up through 18.)

☐	A good meal
☐	A technical improvement
☐	Nonsense
☐	A fine
☐	A rubbish heap
☐	A devoted scientist
☐	Blow up an airliner in flight
☐	Burn a heretic at the stake
☐	A short-circuit
☐	"By this ring I thee wed."
☐	A baby
☐	Torture a person in a concentration camp
☐	Love of Nature
☐	A madman
☐	An assembly line
☐	Slavery
☐	A mathematical genius
☐	A uniform

Cross Out Numbers Used:
1 2 3 4 5 6 7 8 9 10 11 12 13 14 15 16 17 18

THE HARTMAN VALUE PROFILE

2 Profile B:
By Robert S. Hartman, Ph.D.

Instructions

As you did in Profile A, list the phrases on Profile B. from BEST to WORST (with the BEST item receiving a "1" and the WORST item receiving an "18").

Here you are looking at the phrases and deciding if:
YOU BELIEVE ___ is
BETTER THAN ___.
You are not doing a descriptive list of what your present condition is like. If you are not employed outside your home or are a student, treat what you do as "work".
Again, do this profile in ONE sitting and be careful to use each number only ONE TIME.

Under no conditions may the results from this profile be the sole source of information for the hiring or dismissal of anyone from or for any job.

After you have finished, please check to make sure that you have used all the numbers from 1 through 18, without repeating any. (Start with your number 1 and find each number up through 18.)

"I like my work — it does me good."

"The universe is a remarkably harmonious system."

"The world makes little sense to me."

"No matter how hard I work, I shall always feel frustrated."

"My working conditions are poor, and ruin my work."

"I feel at home in the world."

"I hate my work."

"My life is messing up the world."

"My work contributes nothing to the world."

"My work brings out the best in me."

"I enjoy being myself."

"I curse the day I was born."

"I love my work."

"The lack of meaning in the universe disturbs me."

"The more I understand my place in the world, the better I get in my work."

"My work makes me unhappy."

"I love the beauty of the world."

"My work adds to the beauty and harmony of the world."

Cross Out Numbers Used:
1 2 3 4 5 6 7 8 9 10 11 12 13 14 15 16 17 18

Practical Implications of Organizational Culture Where Americans and Japanese Work Together

Jill Kleinberg

Japanese firms in the United States currently receive considerable attention from academicians, business practitioners, and the popular press. We are learning that the meeting of Americans and Japanese in the workplace does not necessarily proceed smoothly, in large part because of cultural differences. This article considers the organizational culture that emerges in one specific *binational* setting. It examines the implications of organizational culture for the firm's ability to achieve its goals and discusses solutions to culturally based problems that derive from an ethnographic perspective.

Conceptualizing Culture in Binational Organizations

My interest in Japanese-owned firms in the United States grows out of a personal work experience involving a small team of Japanese and Americans. Despite the fact that we all were knowledgeable regarding the other's society, tensions stemming from different approaches to work beset the work setting. Later, a pilot study focusing on six Japanese firms in the Los Angeles area allowed me to examine more systematically what it is like for Japanese and Americans to work together (Kleinberg 1989).

In the course of asking American and Japanese respondents, in unstructured taped interviews, to talk in detail about their job, I learned that they too found the environment fraught with tension. Furthermore, as interview materials accumulated, it was clear that Americans and Japanese, respectively, recurringly articulated certain concerns. This prompted me to formulate the issue in terms of cultural clash in the workplace. When people talked about those things in the binational setting which were strange and often upsetting, they inadvertently gave insight into the expectations that they brought to the workplace. If expressed with regularity among members of the same societal group, these expectations then could be thought of as "cultural" expectations.

Culture as Cognitive Sketch Maps

Cognitive anthropology (Frake 1983; Goodenough 1981) provides the model that I found most helpful for uncovering and representing American and Japanese cultural expectations about work. *Culture* is defined as the acquired knowledge people use to give order to their world, to interpret their experience and to generate social behavior (Spradley 1979). Cultural knowledge is widely shared by a group of people, it is distinctive to the group, and it is constructed, passed on, and reinforced through social interaction. Cultural knowledge may be explicit, or it may reflect the tacit assumptions that many consider to be the innermost core of culture.

Culture is viewed as a dynamic process. The metaphor of *cognitive sketch map*, borrowed from Frake, best captures the understanding of culture which I gained from fieldwork in binational firms. As Frake explains, "People are cast out into imperfectly charted, continually shifting seas of everyday life. Mapping them out is a constant process resulting not in an individual cognitive map, but in a whole chart case of rough, improvised, continually revised sketch maps" (Frake 1977:6–7, quoted in Spradley 1979:7).

My research relies on a kind of content analysis known as *domain analysis* (Spradley 1979, 1980) to discover underlying cultural knowledge. It is inferred from people's verbal utterances, from their observed behaviors, and from the material artifacts that they use. Domain analysis seeks to discover categories (domains) and subcategories of cultural knowledge, as well as cultural themes, or broad cognitive principles that recur in a number of domains. The following section illustrates both the concept of cognitive sketch map and the process of discovery.

Nation-Specific Work Sketch Maps

Domain analysis of the pilot study interviews resulted in a partial representation of what I term *nation-specific work sketch maps*. Work sketch maps encompass a broad range of cultural assumptions. For example, they reflect a group's idea of such things as: what it means to be a superior or a subordinate; how responsibility and authority should be expressed; and the way to go about getting a job done. In any society, work sketch maps grow out of people's experience as members of the society and their experience in work organizations.

Much of the uneasiness in the binational setting resulted from differences in the American and Japanese "concept of the job" (Figure 1). Each group dwelled on this theme of the job, but each mapped the terrain differently. In particular, friction developed between the way Americans mapped the domain of cultural knowledge "concept of position" and the way Japanese managers mapped the domain "shape of one's responsibility." Americans wanted to clearly define the parameters of their job, as well as achieve the correspondence among their title, their responsibilities, their authority, and the pay that they expected from working in a particular U.S. industry. The Japanese, in contrast, emphasized flexibility in responsibility—with regard to the allocation of tasks and the range of action that one takes to do a job; they even viewed helping to develop one's coworkers as a constituent aspect of responsibility.

CONCEPT OF THE JOB

"Americans"

Concept Of Position

    Demarcated parameters
    Correspondence among title,
    duties, rights, and pay

Relationship Among Responsibility,
Authority, And Risk

"Japanese"

Concept Of Position

    Place in that company
    Orderly career path

Shape Of One's Responsibility
    Flexibility of action
    Responsibility for coworkers
    Flexibility in task allocation

Balancing Self/Group Interests

Figure 1. Sketch maps regarding the concept-of-the-job theme (adapted from Kleinberg 1989) Categories of cultural knowledge are indicated as follows: all letters capitalized = theme; first letter of word capitalized = domain; underlined = subdomain.

These aspects of American and Japanese work sketch maps became problematical, from the American perspective, because formal and informal work arrangements in binational firms diverged in critical ways from those in American firms. Most "binationals" in my sample, for instance, did not provide employees with formal job descriptions or, if they did, the descriptions showed little resemblance to those of past experience. The following excerpt gives a sense of a common response to this situation. It also illustrates the kind of utterances from which cultural assumptions were inferred.

> If you look at some of these responsibilities [of coworkers] . . . I mean, some of these guys are responsible for Pluto and Mars. Anything. I mean, whatever you want it to be. This is the first corporation I've worked at where employees write their own job descriptions. . . . The [Japanese] manager says, "I need a person to do this type of job," and you hire the person and that becomes his job description. I look at some of these job descriptions and I say, "What is the job description for *this* position, for *that* position?" Not what the guy perceives it is. What actually is it?

In many cases, an American worked hard to negotiate a clear definition of the job, ideally one that reflected conventional job categories—the "this position" and "that position" referred to in the above quote—only to find that the Japanese boss paid no heed to it. In fact, when Americans expressed their discomfort, it only reinforced Japanese managers' emphasis on flexibility of responsibility.

Emergent Organizational Culture(s)

The binational is new terrain for both Americans and Japanese. Nevertheless, each brings the old chart case of cognitive sketch maps to navigate the work setting. To fully comprehend the organizational consequences of clash in nation-specific assumptions about work, the applied anthropologist must consider the emergent organizational culture. My understanding of the importance of organizational culture crystallized during one year of intensive fieldwork in one of the pilot-study firms. The company is called here LASCO (Los Angeles Subsidiary Company). A brief description of LASCO highlights the conditions that influenced the way members made sense of the setting.

LASCO was a leading player in the multiunit, multination "computer peripherals group" of a major Japanese trading company. Fieldwork occurred during a time of remarkable expansion, in both profits and the number of employees. As in other binationals in the pilot study, the Japanese dominated. The president, who adopted the American name Matt, was Japanese, as were almost all persons in key management positions. Some 15 in number, these Japanese, or *chuzaiin,* had been sent from the Tokyo headquarters for assignments of usually around five years. All were long-

"Americans"

LASCO IS DIFFERENT
   Jobs Lack Clarity
   No Correspondence Among Title,
      Duties, Authority, And Pay

LIMITED OPPORTUNITY
   No Career Path
   Ceiling On Advancement
   Shut Out Of Information Flow
      And Decision Making

"Japanese"

LASCO INSEPARABLE FROM
   TRADING COMPANY
   LASCO Strategy Part Of
   Peripherals Group Strategy

MANAGING LASCO
   Americans Are A Problem
      Inflexibility
      Narrow interpretation of responsibility
      Concern for power and money
      Self-interest above group welfare

Competition For Control Of
   Business Group

Structure Reflects Strategic Goals
   And Individual Capability
      Reorganize whenever appropriate
      Japanese most capable of strategic
        management
      Separate Japanese and Americans

Career And Personal Identity Tied To LASCO
   How to succeed at LASCO
      Please both Matt and Tokyo
      Get job done
      Avoid mistakes

Figure 2. Major subgroup cultures. Categories of cultural knowledge are indicated as in Figure 1; in addition, italics = sub-subdomain.

term members of the trading company. Locally hired employees, the "Americans" as opposed to the "Japanese" in a language convention of the company, were of diverse national and ethnic origin. The 20 or so who were managers were mainstream Caucasians or Japanese Americans.

Domain analysis of the doings and sayings of organizational members, not surprisingly, revealed the existence of two strong subcultural groupings emerging around the "Japanese" and the "Americans" (Figure 2). A brief overview of the way these subgroups mapped the binational terrain shows the importance of nation-specific work sketch maps in shaping their respective understandings. (See Kleinberg 1991 for a more detailed description of LASCO's organizational cultures.)

Understandings that were widely and exclusively shared among the Americans entirely grew out of frustrated expectations. Jobs at LASCO not only lacked clarity, but the normal correspondences among title, responsibilities, authority, and pay were missing. Americans, moreover, perceived limitations on their opportunities to advance, partly understood in terms of the absence of an orderly career path within the firm and partly understood as a ceiling on how high they would be allowed to advance. Finally, they saw themselves shut out of the flow of information and decision making.

Shared chuzaiin understandings that concerned managing LASCO also emerged largely in response to differences in work sketch maps. Most notable was the notion that Americans are a problem to be managed: they tend to interpret their responsibility too narrowly, to be too concerned with authority and money, and to push for their own interests over those of the work group or company. Certain understandings comprising the notion that structure should reflect strategic goals and individual capability also arose from perceived cultural differences—in particular, the assumption that the Japanese are most capable of strategic management and the as-

WE ARE UNIQUE	CHANGE IS A CONSTANT	WE ARE A COMPANY DIVIDED
Attempting Something Extraordinary	New People	"Japanese"
Japanese and Americans working together	Chuzaiin	Status (position, assignment, information, influence)
Unusual strategy	Japanese visitors	Relationship to the firm (pay, benefits, and independence)
	Local hires	Way of thinking
Special Challenges	Reorganization	"American"
Communication gap	Restructuring subdivisions	Status (position, assignment, information, influence)
Cultural gap	Reassignment to work groups	Relationship to the firm (pay, benefits, and independence)
	New reporting relationships	Way of thinking

Figure 3. Organization-wide culture. Categories of cultural knowledge are indicated as in Figure 1.

sumption that Japanese and Americans should be separated as much as possible through the organizational structure.

Going almost daily to LASCO, I was most cognizant of the subgroup cultures. The richness of the organization-wide culture—that set of understandings shared by Americans and Japanese—became evident during data analysis after fieldwork had ended. Still, the organization-wide culture also overwhelmingly reflected awareness of LASCO's binational, bicultural nature (Figure 3).

Members commonly understood their binational, bicultural organization as being unique. They shared the knowledge of constant change emanating from the coming and going of chuzaiin and Japanese visitors, as well as from the influx of new Americans. They shared also the knowledge that LASCO was a company divided into two social categories, with "Japanese" and "Americans" distinguished by differences in status, the nature of their relationship to the firm, and their respective ways of thinking.

Reorganization as a Vehicle for Illustrating Emergent Culture

No phenomenon better illustrates the process by which cultural understandings emerged at LASCO than the frequent restructuring that occurred. "Reorganization" constituted an important part of organizational members' cognitive sketch maps regarding change. The description of reorganization which follows helps clarify (1) the interconnection among work sketch maps, subgroup cultures, and the organization-wide culture, and (2) some problematic aspects of LASCO that the applied anthropologist might target in organizational consulting. Any particular reorganization meant some or all of the following for LASCO's members: restructuring of subdivisions; reassignment of individuals to new work groups with, probably, new task assignments; and new reporting relationships (see Figure 3). Beyond this common framework, however, Americans and Japanese viewed the phenomenon differently.

For LASCO's chuzaiin managers, reorganization expressed the subgroup assumption that organizational structure should reflect strategic goals and individual abilities (Figure 2). Matt articulated this in his philosophy of organization:

> The Japanese way of organization, of operating is: the organization is secondary. The point is, who is the person, the individual now working? . . . The American way is the organization chart. It is like hiring a pre-fixed box on the organization chart. In Japan, the person is first, and then you make the box under him. . . . *Job descriptions and responsibilities are only based on the person, not on the box.* [emphasis added]

Chuzaiin assumed that the form reorganization would take ultimately was Matt's decision, though they might seek to influence events. Americans assumed simply that it was a "Japanese" decision. A chuzaiin sometimes hoped for a certain assignment; nevertheless, chuzaiin understood that their trading company career hinged more on their general earnestness, cooperativeness,.and competency than on their specific position.

Japanese flexibility in organization allowed a distribution of responsibility and authority across individual job slots which was quite alien to Americans. One reorganization, for instance, among other changes, transferred several Americans from the Marketing Group to two product sales groups, thereby diffusing marketing functions across work groups. For the Americans, this resulted in ambiguity about who was supposed to do what and who had authority to make decisions—even regarding something as simple as organizing LASCO's booth at a trade fair.

The change, in (Japanese) management's view, enhanced the respective product groups' responsiveness to the market. It also reflected management's assessment of the American in charge of the Marketing Group. One chuzaiin described the group manager in this way:

> We like George's attitude and capability. He's very aggressive. He can take very quick action. That's what I like. . . . One missing point is lack of ability of organizing people, managing the people, making the organization work efficiently.

I observed this American group manager gradually devote more of his time to the role of "internal consultant" regarding new product development. It was a role for which he was eminently qualified, and it relieved him of responsibility for managing people. In the American context, the ambiguity in organizational arrangements surrounding this case and the emergent, organic nature of responsibility and authority would be symptoms of poor management. Among chuzaiin, these arrangements make sense if people have the proper spirit and skills for cooperation.

The issue of how Americans demonstrate that they are capable of handling responsibility and leadership is a critical one in the binational setting. Americans must establish trust with their chuzaiin coworkers, and trust develops only with time; it is an elongated developmental perspective difficult for most Americans to comprehend. As a sales manager in the binational's Printer Group explained, he and the Japanese group manager "had to develop our friendly attitudes in order to accomplish the communication." These friendly attitudes were the key to gaining position and responsibility and, very importantly, information.

> I think that, at least within this organization, you have to earn your position. You are not given responsibility. You earn your responsibility. Therefore, you must display your trust[worthiness], your willingness to work, your devotion to the company. And, once you have accomplished that, then the information, and the amount of information you get, just keeps going up.

Rapport among members of the Printer Group was extremely good— at least before a reorganization radically changed the group's size and composition—largely because of the group manager's tremendous effort to build a sense of belongingness (see Kleinberg 1993). In other chuzaiin-managed groups, intercultural trust was not evident. Critical information frequently did not reach Americans, nor did Americans enjoy the level of re-sponsibility characteristic of this work group.

The practice of sharing strategic information almost exclusively among Japanese reflected the chuzaiin subgroup's assumption that only they are capable of strategic management (Figure 2). So did the practice, in successive reorganizations, of placing key positions that involved com-munication with Japan under Japanese stewardship. In the absence of a shared mindset—with regard to a generalized business culture, and to hu-man relations in general—sufficient trust cannot develop.

An excerpt from a conversation with a chuzaiin illustrates the impor-tance of cultural literacy. It also gives insight into the chuzaiin assumption that ideally Americans and Japanese should occupy separate spheres at LASCO (Figure 2).

> In some sense, Japanese society is very emotional, and it is a human relations society. In Western countries, the principle of the contract is the basis. In Japan, a guy has many relations with many people, and their role overlaps. This is a big difference with the American organization; so it is not easy to adjust. . . .
> This is the point. We Japanese can get detailed information from Japanese vendors because of language and culture. We can speak with the Japanese frankly and friendly. But on the other hand, in the case of the U.S., the Americans are more sensitive to what Americans are thinking and feeling. So, Americans should be in charge of the American side, and Japanese of the Japanese side.

The next several paragraphs examine reorganization as American em-ployees experienced it. Some American veterans of reorganization, usually people in line positions, saw the rationale for each one in retrospect. None-theless, Americans criticized the resulting ambiguity. One veteran ex-plained:

> But the method, the way the changes are handled, is difficult. . . . It's just that the people themselves are never given explanations for why those changes are being done. That makes it difficult to adjust to them. . . . The problem is, *you don't know where you fit in,* and so, consequently, *You don't know if you're looked at positive[ly] or negative[ly] because of the change.* [emphasis added]

Most Americans, in fact, resented the dearth of reliable information about when and what changes would occur, their inability to evaluate the meaning of their new position in the company status system, and their fre-quent confusion over what they were supposed to be doing even after they started a new job. The following excerpt from a conversation with two mar-keting specialists who had just learned that a reorganization would move them from the Marketing Group to the Printer Group illustrates a common response. Their remarks also indicate how they conceptualized their jobs in contrast to chuzaiin jobs.

Specialist #1: [*Sarcastically*] See, everyone knows about it but us.
Specialist #2: Mainly I'm disappointed in George [the boss]. He should have been the one to tell us. . . . That is his responsibility. [They heard instead from the Japanese manager of the Printer Group.]
Specialist #1: We don't know whether or not there is going to be any problem with this. Maybe there will be. We [Marketing and Printer Groups] don't always do things the same way. . . .
Specialist #1: When we [Americans] specialize, there's a reason for it. . . . We don't like to be just pushed into something that may not be what we do.
Specialist #2: We're not animals to be moved around at someone's whim. . . . They [the Japanese] see nothing wrong with this.
Specialist #1: They don't think anything of it. They stay in a job a year or so and then are moved. But we're not used to that. . . .
Specialist #1: We would like to have the feeling that we have some control over our lives.

Rumor long preceded any official announcement. Moreover, management often iterated several successive versions of the form and timing of reorganization. The comments of the (American) personnel manager about a major restructuring subsequent to the one involving the marketing specialists quoted above capture the phenomenon's elusiveness:

Personnel manager: Nothing is announced yet about the reorganization of course. I guess Components, Marketing, and Printer [Groups] are being combined. I heard it from Ken Sasaki [chuzaiin head of the Printer Group]. It looks like we're staying here though. We renewed the lease until June of next year. Terry Shimizu [chuzaiin head of the Administration Group] told me. . . .
Ethnographer: Is it general knowledge already?
Personnel manager: I believe all the people involved in the transfers are aware, but I don't know for sure. . . .
Ethnographer: Terry [Shimizu] didn't go over it with you?
Personnel manager: No. A lot of these changes just happened though, I can tell . . . They [the chuzaiin] don't know until it happens. They've been running around like crazy for the last week—three weeks. . . . They're still doing a lot of talking. . . .
Ethnographer: Tell me again what the new group will be called?
Personnel manager: Yesterday I heard "OEM Sales." Today I don't know. It wasn't definite. . . . I spent the last two days updating my record books—salary, according to departments. Now it all has to be done again. Why doesn't someone just say? . . . It's awful when people [Americans] come to me. They assume I know, and I don't. . . . I don't feel that I should be involved in the business structure of the company, *but when it comes to moving people around from one type of position to another, I feel I have valuable input.* [emphasis added]

Applying Ethnographic Insights

LASCO obviously had significant organizational problems, many of which are best understood from a cultural perspective. The prominent subcultural groupings of Americans and Japanese conflicted in important areas. One group's shared understandings largely emerged in negative response to behavior of the other group's members. Both behavior and response reflected nation-specific work sketch maps. Organization-wide assumptions provided some sense of unity, but not enough to overcome the we-versus-they dichotomy between Americans and Japanese that was expressed at both subgroup and organization-wide levels.

This emphasis on problems overlooks the fact that many organizational members at times enjoyed the challenges of the work setting. Camaraderie could exist between Americans and Japanese, as many instances of mutual joking attested. Some people, especially those whose work required little cross-cultural interaction, avoided the worst of the cross-cultural tensions. Nonetheless, the cognitive sketch maps that emphasized separateness or otherness were widespread. People pulled them from their chart case for navigation and used them whenever circumstances seem appropriate, particularly during times of stress.

This conflicting sense making had serious implications for those interrelated organizational outcomes that concern management. I refer to such outcomes as: meeting the organization's productivity objectives; job satisfaction, in part reflected in absenteeism and turnover; and individual growth (see McCaskey 1983; Staw 1984). Satisfaction and individual growth were a problem, especially for Americans, given the ambiguities of the work setting and their limited opportunity to exercise responsibility and leadership. Seeing chuzaiin occupy the important positions and seeing any hope of a systematic job sequence obliterated by the idiosyncratic pattern of reorganization, furthermore, removed powerful incentives for Americans to put forth their best effort. Absence of incentive was compounded by a prevailing sense of risk caused by the lack of job clarity and information; for many Americans, under such conditions, inaction often seemed the best response. I observed hours of work lost as Americans complained among themselves. Although I do not have information about absenteeism, turnover was high by area standards, in the one year I was able to track it.

LASCO's members, from Matt on down, recognized that culture had organizational consequences, although they are thinking exclusively of national culture. The theme that "we are unique," which emerged at the organization-wide level, obviously reflected such recognition. Nonetheless, management never had attempted systematically to integrate an awareness of culture—national or organizational—into its management practices. One reason was that LASCO was sales driven. Pursuing daily business in the ever-changing computer electronics industry took priority. Just as important, however, was the fuzziness of the culture concept. Organizational members did not have the tools for visualizing culture, or for visualizing the process by which culture affects organizational outcomes. This is where an ethnographic perspective is particularly valuable.

Intercultural Education and Training

In my experience, most binational firms that turn to an outside consultant for help with problems defined as "cultural" seek either cross-cultural education or cross-cultural training. Cross-cultural education often involves seminars about Japanese society and organizational behavior for Americans, or about American society and organizational behavior for Japanese employees. An intercultural communications paradigm (see, for example, Adler 1991 and Samovar et al. 1981) implicitly underlies cross-cultural education.

The paradigm encompasses recognition that deeply rooted assumptions in the societal or business culture color our perception of people and events. When confronted with behaviors that are unfamiliar, especially behaviors that violate our notion of common sense or propriety, we usually react by forming a negative attitude regarding the intentions and capabilities of the cultural other. The paradigm thus emphasizes knowing one's own culture in addition to knowing the "foreign" culture. Knowledge imparted through cross-cultural education efforts aims at promoting mutual understanding with the hope of improving the organizational climate.

Cross-cultural training, on the other hand, represents an active "intervention" characteristic of the scholarly and professional field of organization development (OD). OD can be defined as "a process by which behavioral science knowledge and practices are used to help organizations achieve greater effectiveness, including improved quality of work life and increased productivity" (Huse and Cummings 1985:1). Cross-cultural training falls into the category of human-process interventions that target the people within organizations and their interaction processes (Huse and Cummings 1985:84). It can focus either on individuals, as does the T-group technique, or on specific work groups.

The intercultural communications model explicitly underlies cross-cultural training efforts. Trainers emphasize skills for effectively analyzing cross-cultural situations in order to avoid negative stereotyping, misperception, and misunderstanding. Apart from a framework for defusing and accommodating problems that arise from cultural clash, cross-cultural training sometimes aims at a framework for creating cultural synergy (Adler 1991; Moran and Harris 1982). This approach views cultural diversity as a resource for developing strategies, structures, and practices that transcend the individual cultures of an organization's members.

The notion of nation-specific work sketch maps introduced here adds an important dimension to cross-cultural training in an organizational setting that is missing from more conventional, etic conceptualizations of work-related values, attitudes, and expectations. (See Adler 1991 and Hofstede 1980 for general approaches, and Ouchi 1981 for an ideal-type comparison of Japanese and American organizational forms.) As a systematic representation of social categories and patterns of thinking, from the native's own perspective, the construct of work sketch maps enables us to visualize concretely what happens when an employee's specific assumptions about work are transgressed by formal and informal organizational arrangements.

To illustrate, recall the situation of the two marketing specialists who were transferred to the Printer Group. It was a situation well suited to a work-group-level OD intervention. The Americans changed groups with resentment and fear. Once in the Printer Group, they experienced ambiguity regarding their work role in relation to that of former coworkers in the Marketing Group. Therefore, their initial trepidation was legitimized, and their perception that LASCO's Japanese management "doesn't know what it is doing" was confirmed.

A cultural mediator, working with the Americans, could uncover the violated assumptions that guided their response. They were, for instance, uneasy because the parameters of their new jobs were unclear; the new jobs did not allow them to perform fully the activities that they associated with their title; and the expected chain of command was missing. Moreover, they felt the risk of failing was great because of these conditions. Working with the Japanese group manager, the mediator could learn that he assumed the company has the right to move people at will; that the changes were to the company's benefit; that people should make the welfare of the company and work group their first priority; and that work need not be divided into clearly bounded territories to proceed effectively. Bringing the Americans and the Japanese group manager together to talk about their differing assumptions and reactions, if done skillfully, could promote understanding, good will, and more effective interactions. The chuzaiin manager could clarify the task behavior he expected from these subordinates and the basis on which they would be evaluated. He could, in addition, coordinate with the Marketing Group manager so there was more clarity about that interface.

The situation, in fact, offers an opportunity for wider "process consultation" (Huse and Cummings 1985:84) involving all members of the group. Most importantly, the mediator or trainer could help the group construct an explicit framework for diagnosing and solving problems that arose, in part, from cultural differences. (The same problem-solving framework should help members analyze and assess the desirability of the emergent culture of the work group.) Cultural accommodation might in fact transform into cultural synergy as, for instance, the chuzaiin manager learned to provide more explicit guidelines for the Americans than he normally would for Japanese subordinates, and the Americans began to feel secure enough within the group to regard responsibility more organically than they have previously.

Organizational Transformation

The impact of cross-cultural training tends to be of limited duration and limited scope; certain individuals, or work groups, may benefit for a period of time. But the culturally based problems of a company like LASCO are systemic. Long-lasting solutions hinge on organizational-level change.

Organizational-level interventions aimed at changing the *corporate culture* have been an OD focus since the 1980s. It is important to note, however, that the dominant practitioner-oriented view of corporate culture exhibits a managementcentric bias (Baba 1989; Smircich and Calas 1987) that emphasizes those organization-wide assumptions that directly relate to achieving an organization's strategic goals (I luse and Cummings 1985; Narayanan and Nath 1992). Furthermore, this view conceptualizes culture as an internal organizational variable that management can manipulate (see Davis 1984 and Kilmann 1984 for illustrations of the model, and Smircich and Calas 1987 for a critique). An holistic, ethnographic perspective enables the applied anthropologist to "diagnose" organizational culture more accurately and visualize a program for change more effectively than prevailing approaches in the OD field.

Ethnographic analysis not only shows the influence subcultural groupings can have on an organization's functioning, it also shows that culture represents a pattern of sense-making that has contours and layers of meaning that go far beyond assumptions that specifically concern strategic goals. Ethnographic analysis also shows that many if not most cultural assumptions emerge spontaneously; they are interactively constructed, often in response to circumstances over which management exerts no control. Change efforts must focus broadly on creating conditions that foster a system of meaning conducive to productivity, satisfaction, and individual growth, keeping in mind that culture cannot be changed directly nor can the results of change efforts be predicted absolutely (McCaskey 1983).

How then, once an organization is found to have problems manifested in its cultural configuration, can we approach the task of transforming culture in the desired direction? The OD literature provides useful guidelines, despite the fact that commonly used diagnostic techniques reveal primarily management-centered assumptions regarding "how we do things around here" and, consequently, the results of change efforts are too often superficial.

OD specialists advise, for instance (Huse and Cummings 1985:357–358), that: (1) change should start from a clear vision of the organization's strategy and of the shared patterns of thought and action needed to make this strategy work; (2) top management must be committed to the change effort; (3) the actions of senior executives should symbolize and, thus, communicate the desired assumptions and behaviors; (4) modifications in organizational structure, human resource systems, information and control systems, and management styles must support the desired cultural transformation; and (5) organizational members should be selected and socialized (and, according to Huse and Cummings, terminated) to achieve a fit with the desired culture.

Action Plan for LASCO

LASCO's top executives shared a clear vision of the firm's business objectives. Their vision lacked, however, a clear idea of the human-resource dimension of a strategy for achieving these objectives. The general action plan that I propose aims at building a culture of mutual trust between Americans and Japanese so that they can transcend the bounds of their respective nation-specific work sketch maps. My suggestions involve the following.

Instilling an Official Ideology

That part of the organization-wide culture which emphasized LASCO's uniqueness (Figure 3) reflected employees' pride in the company and a sense of unity, despite the underlying awareness of cultural differences. In very Japanese fashion (see Rohlen 1974), Matt consciously instilled this philosophy of uniqueness and belongingness through speeches given on ceremonial occasions and when he occasionally addressed product work groups. He talked schematically about the history and strategic goals of the trading company, of LASCO, and of the computer peripherals group; he talked, albeit vaguely, about the challenges of having Americans and Japanese work together; he used the metaphor of family to represent the closeness and cooperativeness among organizational members which he presents as the ideal for LASCO.

I propose supplementing these efforts by more systematic socialization of employees—through orientations for new recruits and cross-cultural education seminars or workshops ultimately involving all employees. Formal socialization should emphasize (1) detailed knowledge of the wider organizational context of the trading company, particularly for the Americans, and (2) cross-national differences in societal and business cultures. While chuzaiin generally knew something about American society and business practices, they did not understand the work sketch maps that guided American thought and behavior. Few American employees knew much about Japan and the Japanese beyond the most common stereotypes. Such knowledge would do much to demystify the strange and frustrating aspects of LASCO. Furthermore, it would facilitate development of a sense of unity and pride in the unique binational organization.

Distributing Work and Information

No matter how strongly management expresses an official philosophy of uniqueness, extensive modification of patterns for distributing both work and information is required for LASCO's culture to change toward one more conducive to organizational unity and effectiveness. Many binationals see the answer to their cultural conflicts in a process they term *Americanization* or *localization.* Generally, this means instituting formal structures and human-resource systems common to American firms, as well as placing more Americans in upper-level management positions.

LASCO's localization efforts, imperfectly realized, had centered on the long-range policy of establishing product-specific subsidiaries run in the American way by Americans. The top executive of each existing subsidiary was Japanese however. At LASCO itself, the personnel manager had been instructed to evaluate every locally hired employee's job in order to facilitate reordering the jumble of idiosyncratic job titles and job descriptions (where they existed) into a system of job categories, job descriptions, and pay levels that conformed to American industry standards.

Americanizing the form of management structures and systems might help Americans feel more comfortable, as well as hopeful that the firm offered a logical job sequence. Such standardization would be effective especially among nonmanagerial employees in jobs that involve limited intercultural contact. But this alone is not the answer. At LASCO, and probably most binational firms, nation-specific work sketch maps still would guide the informal, everyday behavior of chuzaiin and Americans despite the formal systems. The meaning that the company has for its members, therefore, would continue to be defined by competing subgroup cultures and an organization-wide culture that primarily expressed awareness of differences.

Management needs consciously to rethink work tasks so that the dichotomy between "Japanese" and "American" jobs disappears. The goal should be considerable sharing of responsibility, authority, and therefore, information among Americans and Japanese. Americans' general perception that they are outside the flow of information found justification in the observed pattern of communication at LASCO. One saw all Japanese meetings taking place throughout the day. Chuzaiin usually went together to a nearby Japanese restaurant for lunch and stayed after the workday officially ended to talk some more. If Americans are to be integrated into jobs that span the U.S.- and Japan-related dimensions of the business, strategic information must be shared with them. More timely and reliable information about impending reorganizations, moreover, would help reduce Americans' insecurity and resentment concerning this phenomenon. It is extremely important for top management to formalize mechanisms for sharing information.

Furthermore, Americans must be given the opportunity to achieve cultural literacy with regard to Japanese, or trading company, organizational behavior. Cultural literacy builds as Americans become integrated into the line of communication with Japan.

LASCO's Printer Group serves as a model for how this can be accomplished at the work-group level (Kleinberg 1993). Under the guidance of the Japanese manager, this group evolved practices that tied Americans closely to Japanese counterparts in Tokyo. Americans established regular telex and fax communication with Tokyo (not allowed by most Japanese group managers unless the local employee spoke fluent Japanese); they joined business meetings and evening entertainment when their Tokyo contacts visited LASCO; and some Americans visited Japan on business trips. Communication with Japan, therefore, represented one of the areas of personal growth for Americans. Moreover, as the individual Americans gained knowledge of the wider organization, the group manager allowed them ever-broader responsibility, backed, as noted earlier, by critical information. Core group members eventually performed tasks that transcended narrowly conceived job categories; several moved into areas of responsibility that were new and challenging. Cross-cultural literacy enabled trust to develop among Japanese manager and American subordinates. Trust facilitated cultural synergy.

Intercultural Training

Intercultural training would build on the knowledge employees gained from cross-cultural education programs and increased cross-cultural literacy through information sharing. Ideally, such training should be done on an ongoing basis, targeting both individuals and work groups. In addition, key persons in the organization, such as the president, heads of work groups, and the personnel manager, should receive special training. The personnel manager, always an American at LASCO, is in an especially critical position. Two different persons held the job during my fieldwork; the first exacerbated cultural tension by obviously identifying with the Americans, and the second facilitated understanding. This position should be formally set up to involve cultural mediation and integration, and a highly qualified person should be hired to fill it.

Hiring

LASCO needs an articulated philosophy with regard to recruiting people who fit the company. The ambitiously career-minded American superstar, for instance, is not a good match. The best match, American or chuzaiin, is someone who is curious, flexible in his or her thinking, willing to take initiative, patient, and more interested in the content of work than formal position. The personnel specialist must make this philosophy clear to group managers and others involved in hiring Americans. The Japanese especially need help in acquiring the skills for evaluating prospective American employees. Personnel staff, additionally, should carefully discuss with potential recruits the circumstances that make a particular personality profile optimum. (Chuzaiin selection, more than it presently does, should consider ability to work with Americans; this means assessing personality, host-country knowledge, and language skills.)

During my observation of LASCO, the Printer Group manager hired an American fresh out of college with the mutual understanding that his relationship with the firm would be "Japanese" in nature (Kleinberg 1993). The group manager planned to mentor the young man through a long-term, learn-by-doing work experience. The American eventually could expect to have extended assignments in Japan. More hiring of this sort gradually would bridge the cultural gap.

Discussion

The proposed actions create conditions that would alter the way organizational members make sense of LASCO. Japanese and American subgroup cultures undoubtedly would continue to exist, but their constituent sketch maps should place less emphasis on immutable differences between the two groups. Assumptions that reflect the new terrain of more open access to information, responsibility, and authority gradually would supercede previously held assumptions at both the subgroup and organization-wide level.

Even if implemented in their entirety, however, these actions cannot fully solve LASCO's problems. Nation-specific work sketch maps reflect core assumptions that are not easily moderated. Moreover, chuzaiin managers undoubtedly will dominate LASCO for some time, thus maintaining to some degree the power inequities that shaped the present cultural configuration. Finally, it is unrealistic to expect that the phenomenon of reorganization, which has had a strong and largely negative impact on the emergent organizational culture, will cease. Not only does the pace of the computer electronics industry favor frequent structural modification, but chuzaiin share a sketch map for reorganization crystallized in prior trading company experience.

It is the applied anthropologist's hope that over time the action plan would foster a high degree of mutual trust between Americans and Japanese. Trust can overcome the barriers formerly defined by differences in nation-specific work sketch maps and reinforced by the strains of frequent reorganization.

References Cited

Adler, Nancy J.
  1991 International Dimensions of Organizational Behavior. Boston: Kent Publishing.

Baba, Marietta L.
   1989   Organizational Culture: Revisiting the Small-Society Metaphor. Anthropology of
      Work Review 10(3):7–10.
Davis, Stanley M.
   1984   Managing Corporate Culture. Cambridge, MA: Ballinger.
Frake, Charles O.
   1977   Plying Frames Can Be Dangerous: Some Reflections on Methodology in Cognitive
      Anthropology. Quarterly Newsletter of the Institute for Comparative Human Development
      1(3):1–7.
   1983   Ethnography. In Contemporary Field Research. R. E. Emerson, ed. Pp. 173–189.
      Prospect Heights, IL: Waveland Press.
Goodenough, Ward H.
   1981   Culture, Language, and Society. Menlo Park, CA: Benjamin/Cummings.
Hofstede, Geert
   1980   Culture's Consequences: International Differences in Work-Related Values. Beverly
      Hills: Sage Publications.
Huse, Edgar F., and Thomas G. Cummings
   1985   Organization Development and Change. St. Paul, MN: West Publishing.
Kilmann, Ralph H.
   1984.   Beyond the Quick Fix. San Francisco: Jossey-Bass.
Kleinberg, Jill
   1989   Cultural Clash between Managers: America's Japanese Firms. In Advances in
      International Comparative Management, Vol. 4. S. B. Prasad, ed. Pp. 221–243. Green-
      wich, CT: JAI Press.
   1991   Organizational Culture in a Binational Setting. Paper presented at the 8th Interna-
      tional Standing Conference on Organizational Symbolism Meeting, Copenhagen, Den-
      mark, June.
   1993   The Crazy Group: Emergent Culture in a Binational Work Group. Paper presented
      at the Association for Japanese Business Studies Meeting, New York, January.
McCaskey, Michael B.
   1983   A Framework for Analyzing Work Groups. In Managing Behavior in Organizations:
      Text, Cases, Readings. L. A. Schlesinger, R. G. Eccles, and J. J. Gabarro, eds. Pp. 4–24.
      New York: McGraw-Hill.
Moran, Robert T., and Philip R. Harris
   1982   Managing Cultural Synergy. Houston: Gulf Publishing.
Narayanan, V. K., and Raghu Nath
   1992   Organization Theory: A Strategic Approach. Homewood, IL: Irwin.
Ouchi, William G.
   1981   Theory Z: How American Business Can Meet the Japanese Challenge. Reading,
      MA: Addison-Wesley.
Rohlen, Thomas P.
   1974   For Harmony and Strength: White-Collar Organization in Anthropological Perspec-
      tive. Berkeley: University of California Press.
Samovar, Larry A., Richard E. Porter, and Nemi C. Jain
   1981   Understanding Intercultural Communication. Belmont, CA: Wadsworth Publishing.
Smircich, Linda, and Marta B. Calas
   1987   Organizational Culture: A Critical Assessment. In Handbook of Organizational
      Communication. F. M. Jablin, L. L. Putnam, K. H. Roberts, and L. W. Porter, eds. Pp.
      228–263. Newbury Park, CA: Sage Publications.
Spradley, James P.
   1979   The Ethnographic Interview. New York: Holt, Rinehart & Winston.
   1980   Participant Observation. New York: Holt, Rinehart & Winston.
Staw, Barry M.
   1984   Organizational Behavior: A Review and Reformulation of the Field's Outcome
      Variables. Annual Review of Psychology 35:627–666.

Change, Loss, and Organizational Culture: Anthropological Consultant as Facilitator of Grief Work

Howard F. Stein

This chapter conceptualizes culture as a sense of "us" created and sustained by shared, common experiences, marked by identifiers (values, meanings, roles, rituals), and expressed in group boundaries that distinguish and differentiate each "us" from "them." Grief, together with powerful defenses against experiencing the pain of grief, results from loss of boundaries when culture changes. This process occurs not only within tribal and national units, and in their "ghost dances" (La Barre 1972) and "nationalistic movements" (Koenigsberg 1975, 1977) to revive the dead and reverse the sense of separateness, but as well in American occupational and other voluntary corporate organizations. In this chapter, I (a) provide a theoretical account of culture and the role of loss and grief; (b) offer a methodological framework for helping organizations undergoing loss and bereavement; and (c) give brief ethnographic vignettes from my consulting work in which culture change, loss, and grief were at play.

At one level, this chapter addresses the question, "What can an organizational anthropologist do in the role of consultant for an organization that is undergoing massive change and grief over loss?" I shall attempt to operationalize the dos and don'ts for practitioners working with organizations, while at the same time doing justice to cultural complexity, to a holistic attitude toward all cultural problems, and to a recognition of the depths of human loss and grief. All my consulting is a species of fieldwork. At another level, it asks the question, "How can one study and develop theory from a culture while one serves as project manager, consultant, interpreter, or change agent?" How can one monitor, describe, interpret, and develop theory from a group in which one is up to one's emotional neck participating? The question "What is culture?" is illuminated by working with people experiencing the triad of change, loss, and grief.

The subject of this chapter is simultaneously my discovery of the importance of grief in many organizations and my role as consultant in trying to help those corporate cultures become "unfrozen." I help them to go through grief rather than continue to flee from grief into action or into more rigid bureaucratic hierarchy. It is a study in how practice can drive theory. It is about our common human predicament. It brings change, loss (real and symbolic death), mourning, and the inability to mourn to the center of culture-theory.

This approach to culture in terms of identity, integrity, boundary, change, loss, and grief derives from years of working and consulting with many organizations (Stein 1986, 1988, 1990a, 1990b, 1991). I was not looking for change, loss, and responses to it. Instead, although I went to the "field" invited to help "solve" one problem, I frequently saw other, more fundamental cultural themes, patterns, or unaddressed issues. As I worked with organizations on their self-defined, self-identified ("emic") issues, I frequently discovered, and then helped them to discover, that underlying many manifest organizational difficulties was a recent or remote loss too painful to acknowledge and work through. It haunted present and future alike, even as it had been banished by executive edict or group-enforced silence. The outline and emotional significance of organizational culture is never so clear as when it has been threatened or altogether lost, for instance, as with downsizing (mass layoffs), plant closings, and corporate takeovers and mergers. People will do almost anything to avoid grieving. Much of culture history can be interpreted as a chronic "inability to mourn" (Mitscherlich and Mitscherlich 1975), the transmission of that inability into an obligation upon the next generation(s), and a later repetition of what cannot be relinquished to inert memory. Consider the following brief, and typical, example.

The chief executive officer (CEO) of a medical corporation invited me to help solve two chronic problems: employee evaluations and scheduling meetings. Employees at all levels resented the entire evaluation process, even though they recognized that some system was necessary to evaluate job performance. It was a toxic topic for everyone. Moreover, many people would not come to regularly scheduled meetings. They could rarely agree on a mutually acceptable time for meetings to get cumulative business done. What meetings did occur were lifeless, perfunctory, boring.

By the fourth day of the consultation, it had become clear to everyone that "evaluations" and "meetings" were the proverbial tip-of-the-iceberg, metaphors that condensed the said and the unsaid, present and past. Over the past two years, the corporation had expanded from a single facility to nearly a dozen medical plants, and from a hundred- to a thousand-physician practice. Many admired senior physicians and executives had left during this time, and the company was unable to recruit as junior executives, trainees, and staff the "cream of the crop" that they had been accustomed to attracting during the prior decade. Supervisors and supervisees mistrusted each other; or worse, each side felt betrayed and abandoned by the other, wished that the "other" were someone else: those who had left or those who "should" have been there instead. Mistrust, accusation, withdrawal, avoidance, all were thick scabs over disappointment, feelings of abandonment, loss, and unfelt sadness over the enormity of the change.

On the morning of the third day, the CEO, at an all-day retreat, introduced the image of a jigsaw "puzzle" that her family assembled and reassembled each Christmas. Part of her hope for the retreat was that we could piece together the organizational puzzle, each person contributing his or her piece, and fill in the missing pieces. By the end of the day, many of those present were shedding tears over the losses and unspent grief that had been channeled into mutual recrimination. Both supervisors and supervisees, management and staff, had been projecting upon their counterparts images of those whom they had lost, missed, or were unable to attract. Each was unable to see, to appreciate, to recognize, to accept, the other for who he, she, or they really were. They could only see who they were *not,* who was *not* there, who was *absent.* As the group could openly grieve the changes and losses, they could begin to work together as a group. By the end of the fourth day, the group was able to plan for their next meeting with virtually no effort. Further, the evaluation process could become more realistic because participants, having begun to mourn their losses, could better accept and assess those who were present without confusing the two.

Organizational Culture Concept

Organization is heir to Alexis de Tocqueville's 1830s observation that individualistic Americans eagerly form and join voluntary associations (1945[1835]). In the West, *organization* likewise often connotes adult-recruited occupational ("work") corporations and industries, religious ("church"), ethnic (fraternal, insurance, cultural perpetuation) societies, and political parties. In either event, in this discussion of organizational culture, loss, and grief, I emphasize what it feels like for people to be in a group. Lloyd deMause and Henry Ebel call it a "group-fantasy" (1977; deMause 1982), and Erik Erikson describes it as psychosocial "identity" (1968). Anthropologists have described this at the more conscious level as experiencing membership in a culture. Adult-recruited organizations draw upon symbols, meanings, and affects that have their unrecognized source in our families, our childhood vulnerabilities, and in their derivatives that become structured in our unconscious. Michael Diamond writes that "organizational identity is the totality of repetitive patterns of individual behavior and interpersonal relationships that taken together comprise the unacknowledged meaning of organizational life" (1988:169).

Occupational and other corporate organizations in modern society build upon and become symbolic "objects" of early symbiosis/merger, ambivalent attachment, separation/individuation, oedipal strivings, and sibling conflicts (Diamond 1984, 1988; Diamond and Allcorn 1986; Koenigsberg 1975, 1977). At the unconscious level of internal mental representation (inner meaning) and feelings, a person stands on the same kind of firm or shaky ground in relation to a workplace organization, as one feels vis-à-vis the solid earth or earthquake-stricken ground. Fantasies and affects around death and separation anxiety which govern a sense of well-being and fear of boundary violation in one's literal foothold, one's ethnic group or nation, also operate in occupational and other outwardly less emotionally vital "secondary" organizations.

Whether we employ culture, identity, or group-fantasy concepts, the emotion-charged image of an organization becomes incorporated as a part of participants' self-images. The organization becomes what Kohut called a "self-object" (1972). Experienced as a reified entity, the organization likewise becomes a vital extension of people's interior life (Larçon and Reitter 1984:345). Organizational symbols, metaphors, and rites express this inner world. Only because of this emotional endowment can the loss of work colleagues and workplaces be so poignant and feel so catastrophic. In our experience of loss in organizations, as in the illness and death of real persons, we lose facets of self and others. The rawness of our wound is a measure of the separation anxiety and other emotions that we experience. These here-and-now experiences rekindle old childhood wounds and feelings, which in turn magnify the present.

Larçon and Reitter describe functions of myths, rites (rituals), and taboos in corporate organizations:

> The business firm, like any other human group, engenders myths, that is, stories about its history. . . . In very broad terms the purpose of the myth is to create—or to support—an ideal image of the firm. This image will cover problematic or obscure aspects and show them in a favorable light. The myth itself creates values. . . .
> Rites are practices which reflect the myth and which have no significance in themselves other than providing an occasion for a consensus on the important problem which the rite masks. . . .
> Taboos can pinpoint the organization's sensitive spots; only those things which strike at the heart of the organization—its basic values, its secret conflict, its contradictions, its traumas—are taboo. Since the taboo is what should be denied, hidden, exorcised, wiped out, it is a fundamental part of the equilibrium of a company. [1984:350–351]

All stories are not myths; all dramatizations are not rituals; all proscriptions (interdictions) are not taboos. Organizational stories, and the occasions on which they are told, do not necessarily mask problems. When groups say and do one thing in order consciously and/or unconsciously not to talk about, feel, or do something else, then such terms as *myth, ritual,* and *taboo* specify the kind of communication taking place.

Mourning and Organizational Culture: Theoretical Issues

Mourning is the fulcrum of change. On one side is working through and liberation. On the other side is the inability to mourn; chronic, often masked, grief that never allows the dead or the lost to be gone; the flight from mourning into repetition; and the endless revitalization or restoration of the past via new generations or recruits (Freud 1957[1917]; Pollock 1977). During the mourning process, individuals and organizations suffering loss engage in constant review of their history (Owen 1986; Stein 1988; Volkan 1981, 1988). Integration of the past is necessary before it can be relinquished and a future emerge uncontaminated by the pull of feelings and fantasies associated with the past. To forget, we must first remember and feel.

Background and Methodology: How Do We Understand, How Do We Help?

My work as organizational consultant falls within the rubrics of the *anthropology of work, applied* and *practicing anthropology*. Doctoral and two decades of subsequent research on ethnicity and adaptation among Slovak- and Rusyn-Americans (Ruthenian-Americans) in the former Steel Valley of western Pennsylvania led me to examine the "New White Ethnic revitalization movement" (Stein and Hill 1977). I have worked during this time with several ethnic fraternal institutions. For the past 14 years, during an annual graduate seminar for occupational medicine clinicians (physicians and physicians' assistants), I have served as individual and group consultant for projects examining the effects of massive layoffs, management and work-force role conflicts, professional and occupational identity issues, influences on midcareer life change, and family influences upon occupational choice, among others. My primary consultations have been with medical academic/training programs.

In the springs of 1983 and 1984, I served as consultant/lecturer at a seminar, "Uncertainty and Management," for Shell International Petroleum Maatschappij B.V. senior executives at the Harvard Business School Conference Center in Mt. Pèlerin, Switzerland. In 1990, I served as a member of a three-person "training/facilitator" team for the retreat of school administrators and school board in a U.S. Great Plains town. During 1990, I was faculty/consultant for a week-long seminar entitled "Ethics in Broadcast News" at the Poynter Institute for Media Studies in St. Petersburg, Florida. In each of these, I requested and received permission to make my own formal presentation(s) fairly late in each sequence, so as first to get to know and become informally known by the group, and to build their cultural context into the very content and style of my own presentation.

I define my consulting role as one in which I (a) am a short-term rather than day-to-day regular participant in the organizational group; (b) am at least to some degree an outsider, if not a stranger (although I might be a regular guest, from weekly to annual); (c) am attempting to learn about and emotionally encompass (Stein 1987b) an organizational cultural system in order to help describe and interpret it to its members, in turn, in order that members of that organizational culture be more knowledgeable of the breadth and depth of their own culture; and (d) am ascribed or assigned little or no formal authority or power position, but acquire my status informally such as through my ability to "network," mediate, or speak with people throughout the organization.

The organizational anthropologist learns about the clients, individual client, or organization not only through naturalistic and participant observation, open-ended as well as focused interviews, and an examination of the "material" culture ranging from documentary sources such as organizational charts and videotapes, to the psychogeography of space-use in the workplace (Stein 1987a; Stein and Niederland 1989), but also most importantly through the "intersubjective resonance of unconscious processes" between anthropologist and client (Odgen 1989:17; see also Modell 1984). Devereux described the anthropologist's subjectivity as the most reliable instrument of ethnographic inquiry (1967). We understand and help others by understanding ourselves, by having emotional as well as cognitive access to others' influence upon us (see Hirschhorn 1988; Hunt 1989; La Barre 1978).

The emotional bond between consultant and organization underlies advisory and strategic skills that one can provide as consultant. Analyst and consultant alike should provide what Winnicott termed a "holding environment" (1965[1963]), symbolic heir to the actual mother's physical holding, her reassuring presence and countenance and reliability that served as "container" for the infant's physically experienced hopes and dreads (Bion 1959). The rhythm of the relationship—building blocks of constancy and trust—is essential to the content.

As organizational anthropologist, I find myself offering a symbolic membrane around those with whom I work by listening deeply for long periods of time. I make room for their worlds within mine, before I say anything (e.g., an interpretation) to them. Within the envelope-like safety of this holding environment, I try to provide them a sense of being heard, being seen, and being understood. This deep recognition is often reciprocated by others in the group. I come to feel enclosed in membranes that they offer in return. Feeling understood, they can tolerate to accept their anxiety and to understand themselves better, and then to extend the gift of empathy to others in the group. Within the mutually constructed safety net of the holding environment, grief begins to be felt, and walls erected against it begin to crumble.

Let me return, then, to the practical question of "What do I do?" in this role. Here, I extrapolate some principles, some dos and don'ts, from my work with organizations (see Table 1 for a schematic). The first is to recognize that group response to change and loss is unconsciously as well as consciously (politically, economically, structurally) organized. It is complex, not neatly packaged. This means that the surface picture presented to the consultant often is a symptom and symbol in which people have an investment because it protects them against pain. Both vertically and horizontally in organizations, people defend against knowing, emotionally as well as cognitively, precisely what they need to know in order to "move on." Client organizations and individuals often do not want to know what they, at some unrecognized level, already know too well. My role becomes that of

Table 1
Dos and Don'ts in Working with Organizations

What To Do	What Not To Do
Listen carefully to many people, in different subunits of the organization.	Don't trivialize or dismiss the identified problem or "presenting complaint," or those who make them.
Track metaphors, silences, verbs, expression of emotion; do a "fantasy analysis" of group process (deMause 1982).	Don't take the presenting problem or issue to be everything, the entire picture.
Build trust.	Don't try to solve the problem prematurely or promise to solve the "wrong" problem.
Give yourself time; ask for more time.	
Use your own emotional responses as cues to organizational experiences.	Don't listen only to one component, person, unit of the organization.
Assume that the presenting complaints, issues, problems are not the whole story.	While you are trying to be efficient, expeditious, helpful to the organization, don't overidentify with the urgency the organization is inducing or projecting into you to solve the problem immediately.
Ask what's been done before to "solve" or address these problems; ask what other types of problems they have had.	Don't say that the problem is only, or "really," one of loss and grief, but that it is a wider or deeper part of the problem initially presented.
Help the organizational group find out what the characteristic problems of the organization are.	Don't overlook the informal structure of authority, status, and decision making; at the same time, don't exclude the formal "chain of command" from your network.
Learn who constitutes the informal authority structure as well as the formal authority structure, and work with both.	
Help the organizational group to understand the complexity, breadth, and depth of their own culture, that in every culture things are not only what they seem; help them to tolerate not knowing for a while, through identification with the consultant's toleration for uncertainty and anxiety.	
Help the organization recognize that responses to change and loss come in many and surprising guises, that people often disguise and rechannel emotional reactions to loss in order to avoid the enormous pain of grief and acceptance of change—and that this resistance is widespread if not "normal" (They're not "crazy" for being like this!)	

mediating between the known and the unknown, the knowable and un-knowable.

Second, while it is essential to elicit and acknowledge the initial view-points presented to the consultant as problems, it is essential not to take them at face value as the necessarily entire "reality." They are starting points. Scott-Stevens writes that:

> The [organizational] consultant must be wary about taking at face value the client's descriptions of the issues at hand. The anthropologist/consultant should already be cognizant of the fact that few people are aware of the details involved in the working of their own culture or subculture. This phenomenon is as true of smaller subcultures, such as groups of people in corporations, as it is of larger societies. [1988:11]

Organizations requesting my consultation have never defined their problem as change, loss, and grief. They have invited me to assist them on some other, concrete, compartmentalized task, problem, or project. Through empathic listening, interpreting, gently confronting, asking questions, and spending time with personnel on their own "turf" throughout the organization, I have discovered repeatedly the role that unspent grief plays in generating the story behind the manifest story. This difficult mutual-discovery process and playful construction (Freud 1964[1937]) violates an almost sacred anthropological tenet that "the native is always right" or "only the native can define and treat or solve his or her problem."

The consultant should convey this methodological approach to the organization. The way one works is to piece together as much of "the whole story" as possible, something that cannot be reduced to the initial presentation of the problem, issue, or task. This approach does not trivialize what one hears. It accords everyone dignity. It also acknowledges that there is more to be pieced together—and that the consultant is there to help precisely with that: to tell the story that has not yet been told, to serve as a liaison between persons and units, and to integrate story lines.

Third, the consultant does not only listen and watch for this story to emerge in others but, through introspection and empathy, constantly monitors his or her own emotional responses to what is being seen and heard, as crucial data about the organization. Some of the most important cues are our own feelings and fantasies. I often either offer a description or interpretation to a group about their own emotional tone or describe my own.

I once consulted with an academic medical department that had a new female director whom many regarded as cold, aloof, even witchlike. As we discussed organizational change, leadership succession, and transition, several people referred to "Peter," whom I later learned to have been her predecessor. Then in the middle of the discussion the new chairperson snapped in reply to another's comment, "You mean Saint Peter." I felt a jolt of surprise, reverence, and awe.

I used my own inner associations aloud (Saint Peter = founder of the Christian church = good father) to inquire into the previous chair's era. He had indeed founded and stabilized the department (being the first outside recruited, long-term chair after a succession of one-year rotating chairs selected from within). He was universally respected as wise, kind, decisive when necessary, but "grandfatherly." He was deeply missed, but his loss had never been mourned. This psychologically made his successor into far more of an ogre than she was. My emotional response to "Saint Peter" was a key to opening up a new level of discussion about the organization's history.

Fourth, the consultant must obtain a good history of the presenting problem and of the organization's problem-solving style. Do not solve the wrong problem or try to solve the correct problem prematurely or alone. Find out what problems have been presented before, by whom, their statuses in the organization, and what has been done and not done. Determine different people's sense of what the problem is, how it developed, and why it has persisted. Find out what the channels of information distribution are, the media used (computers, meetings, memos), and how earlier ideas have been received. In short: What prevented them from working?

Fifth, at least consider presenting problems to be metaphors of larger contextual issues, in addition to real, concrete issues. For instance, in recent years I have been asked to examine, address, and "fix" the following problems that turned out to be vessels that carried the burden of organizations' histories: groups' difficulties scheduling meetings, employee evaluations, factionalism between organizational groups, decreased productivity, poor team morale, conflict between vertical chain of command and horizontal responsibility for carrying out tasks, staff turnover, and role demand. In each of these, I would have missed—and missed the opportunity to help the organization address—the deeper cultural issues, had I failed to pursue the possibility that the "part" first presented to me was metaphoric of a still-elusive "whole."

Vignette 1: From Anniversary Reaction to Organizational Grief

This vignette summarizes seven years of consultation and supervision in a community-based medical corporation that I will call "CMC" (Community Medical Corporation) and that eventually went out of business in June 1985. CMC was one of a half-dozen subsidiaries of a larger company that I will refer to as the main or home office. My official role was to teach, facilitate, and supervise midlevel manager trainees. My unofficial, but valued, role became to help the entire "permanent" chain of command and staff of 25 to navigate two painful, protracted years of uncertainty as to whether CMC would continue, and eventually to help them grieve over the loss of their corporation. After the company closed, five employees (office manager, executive secretary, computer specialist, nurse, medical transcriptionist) were transferred to corporate headquarters. In subsequent years, we discussed and slowly worked through persisting "anniversary reactions" to the painful loss not only of a job but of a way of life that had meaning for those from whom it felt taken away (e.g., offering service to medically underserved and stigmatized populations). Around May and June each year, we found ourselves reminiscing about CMC, still agonizing about why it had to go out of business. Three years ago, while I was talking with the former business (administrative) manager of CMC, she said to me out of the blue:

> I don't think that we ever told you how much we appreciated your continuing to come out every two weeks and visit with us, even after everyone knew that we were closing at the end of June. We were all having lots of strange, uncomfortable feelings during those months, and you were interested in what we were going through. It's not that you had any official information or could do anything about our situation—we were all in the dark for a year or two as to what our fate would be. But you stayed in there with us, down to the very end. I just wanted to tell you we're grateful.

Although she was sitting behind her large wood desk and I was seated at a chair across from her, I felt I had just received a huge hug.

I had driven twice a month to CMC, offering seminars, consultations, and supervision to the eight manager trainees. I had also built up rapport with medical and administrative staff. Officially, I presented a behavioral science conference, seminar, or workshop for 1 to $1\frac{1}{2}$ hours around noon and shadowed clinical trainees with their patients in examining rooms. Unofficially, I helped resolve organizational communication problems between subunits and problems with morale. It made sense from ethnographic, group process, and psychoanalytic method to know and work closely with (emotionally, to encompass; see Stein 1987b) the "whole culture" of the workplace.

Upon such a foundation set since 1979, I began to give even greater attention and sheer time to the personnel of CMC in 1984 and the first half of 1985. I infer by hindsight that I was helping the organizational group to ventilate rage and sorrow, to give feelings and words to their anxiety, to deal with mounting uncertainty over CMC's future, to prepare themselves to relinquish an organizational identity, to be affirmed that they were not "going crazy," to express their confusion over knowing whether to "knuckle down" and get ready to "hold on" to an organization or to start to "let go" and "distance" themselves from it.

One morning I entered the break-room/kitchen/library and noticed several staff members sitting silently—or talking in a hush—with masklike faces, a scene so different from the animated, even loud, din of earlier years. Instead of saying a perfunctory hello and crossing through the group to the seminar room beyond it (where I conducted a formal conference at noon), or instead of going directly to the hallway where exam rooms were and where physicians were likely to be, I poured a cup of coffee, sat down with administrators and staff, often saying nothing, and listened. I would be with them. At first, I might have talked with them about "stress reduction" strategies popular in psychology and organizational consulting. Soon I realized that they most benefited not from specialized tactics of stress reduction (e.g., tightening and relaxing all muscles, one part of the body at a time), but from the fact that I was willing to sit among them, listen empathically, care, occasionally interpret, to help them to feel listened to, heard, acknowledged, and understood rather than be judged, lectured to, or reprimanded. I could relax my urge to do something decisive.

Want of information from the home office and from its most senior executives inflamed and intensified rumor among the program personnel. Scarcity felt like a deliberate withholding. The CEO, vice-CEO, and other upper administrators of the main office emphasized to me, over the final two years of CMC's existence, that they did not want to impose unnecessary emotional burdens on the staff, managers, and trainees of the subsidiary corporation by telling them every detail of what was taking place. One administrator invoked the "no news is good news" aphorism. He later expressed exasperation to me that people in CMC would be so "paranoid" about the home office. Another senior executive from headquarters had visited them earlier and given a stern lecture on "toughing it out," on not being complainers. He reminded them of their obligation to be loyal during difficult times. Several people later said to me that he had not elicited or listened to their worries at all.

Only toward the end of this agonizing waiting did it dawn on me that I was helping them through a chronic crisis, to anticipate and grieve for the eventual loss of an identity—a culture—to deal with unremitting feelings of catastrophe, while continuing to function with trainees and with patients, and act toward the larger community as if nothing were changed (denial). Not only did this profoundly affect them, it did me also. For them, as for me, all this had remained unresolved because none of us—even myself, behavioral science consultant, facilitator, and helper—could ever conclusively, finally, know why it all happened or whether it had to happen. I could only help them, and help myself, to make peace with a past that we had been unable to save or to restore.

This case was my first "teacher" in organizational change, loss, and grief. Its on-the-job training has attuned me to issues of anticipatory grief, grief over actual loss, and the inability to mourn in my work as consultant with organizational cultures. It taught me to trust my own feelings and fantasies evoked as I consult. They serve as valuable, if seemingly ineffable, measures of "something" that an organization is going through and that its members cannot yet put into feelings let alone express in words.

It has also taught me not to ignore my own developmental, emotional tasks, for they are inseparable from my work as consultant. If this 12-year-long case helped me to help people at CMC—people who once "were"

CMC—to say goodbye and to be able to mean and to feel it, then it has also helped me to do likewise. As Searles wrote, therapy, if it is therapeutic to anyone, must be therapeutic to the healer (1975).

Vignette 2: "They're Closing Down My World"

A frequent response to loss and to the threat of loss is the psychological numbing that includes such defenses as splitting, projective identification, externalization, projection, denial, and dehumanizing—simultaneously of others and of aspects of oneself, depriving everyone involved of guilt, shame, and anxiety-inducing pain (Wangh 1986; Nedelmann 1986). One erases any sense of affiliation or obligation toward those who have been lost or those who might be. This occurs in contemporary bureaucratic organizational change such as what is euphemistically called "downsizing" or "RIF" (reduction in force), namely, large-scale layoff of employees (see Tombaugh and White 1990).

For example, at one corporation where 750 workers were laid off and 2000 others were peremptorily transferred or demoted, corporate upper management did little to mitigate the demoralization of the workforce— those forced to leave or those remaining behind. In a callous manner, in public speeches, and in newsletter editorials, the CEO and other policy makers exhorted workers who remained to "take up the slack," to "not let the company down," to learn their new jobs, and to expand their old ones quickly and efficiently so that productivity would not be compromised. Management made no expression of regret or empathy toward those who were forced to leave. Even acknowledgment of remorse at the necessity of the decision, recognition of the workers' and company's loss and grief, and gratitude toward those who were being forced to leave, would have considerably salved the pain of those displaced and of those remaining behind— many of whom saw themselves as "survivors" of a social catastrophe or disaster. Management instead seemed unable even to affirm that anything of emotional significance was happening. Since nothing was lost, there was therefore nothing to mourn. In clinical terms, they sought refuge through what Klein called the "paranoid-schizoid position" in a flight into denial through action (1946).

On a wider cultural note, beyond this organization and overlapping with American culture, it is quintessentially American to respond to loss by denying grief through action in an almost frenetic fashion, pressing for even greater "output." This rush into "doing" (a core American value) represents a reaction formation and counteridentification that protects people against experiencing guilt, anxiety, shame, and identification with the victim. This defense complex, acting in concert with projective defenses, manufactures people into discountable and destructible commodities.

Moreover, upper management at this company quickly began to re-write history, further rationalizing the numbing and discounting of people, by saying that perhaps those people fired had not been needed after all, that this might be an opportunity for the corporation to be rid of some "dead meat" without losing productivity quotas, and the like. Through months of informal consultations with the company's medical staff, I was able to help clinical personnel "decompress" their own sense of horror, outrage, impotence, withdrawal, numbness, guilt over surviving, profound sense of loss, and vacillating identifications with the aggressors and the victims, and to help them to acknowledge that something worthy of grief was in fact taking place.

If only to a small degree, I helped them to rehumanize themselves and those with whom they worked and those whom they treated. I helped them to avow their own frightened and sadness-filled perceptions of their and others' situations, rather than to participate in the masking of organizational history. The implicit role that I sought was to help group members to recognize and feel what might be called the deeper, hidden culture behind the manifest culture that serves largely as defense against anxiety.

Conclusions

In this chapter, I have described my role as anthropological consultant in helping organizational groups to cope with social change and its inevitable losses. The process I have come to facilitate is the difficult work of mourning. Consultation has led me to reflect on its implications for theory of organizational culture, of social change, and of the kinds of interventions that consultants should perform. The practice of applied anthropology has led me to a deeper, disturbing understanding of the common roots and vulnerabilities of all human culture.

Note

Acknowledgments. The author expresses his gratitude to Ann Jordan for her encouragement and perserverance as editor of this bulletin; to Pamela Puntenney for introducing me to NAPA; and to Margaret A. Sheehan for her editorial assistance with this manuscript.

References Cited

Bion, Wilfred R.
  1959 Experiences in Groups. New York: Basic Books.
deMause, Lloyd
  1982 Foundations of Psychohistory. New York: Creative Roots.
deMause, Lloyd, and Henry Ebel, eds.
  1977 Jimmy Carter and American Fantasy: Psychohistorical Explorations. New York: Two Continents/Psychohistory Press.
Devereux, George
  1967 From Anxiety to Method in the Behavioral Sciences. The Hague: Mouton.
Diamond, Michael A.
  1984 Bureaucracy as Externalized Self-System: A View from the Psychological Interior. Administration and Society 16(2):195–214.
  1988 Organizational Identity: A Psychoanalytic Exploration of Organizational Meaning. Administration and Society 20(2):166–190.

Diamond, Michael A., and Seth Allcorn
   1986 Role Formation as Defensive Activity in Bureaucratic Organizations. Political Psychology 7(4):709–732.
Erikson, Erik H.
   1968 Identity: Youth and Crisis. New York: W. W. Norton.
Freud, Sigmund
   1957[1917] Mourning and Melancholia. In The Complete Psychological Works of Sigmund Freud: Standard Edition, Vol. 14. J. Strachey, ed. and trans. Pp. 243–258. London: Hogarth Press.
   1964[1937] Constructions in Analysis. The Complete Psychological Works of Sigmund Freud: Standard Edition, Vol. 23. J. Strachey, ed. and trans. Pp. 255–269. London: Hogarth Press.
Hirschhorn, Larry
   1988 The Workplace Within: Psychodynamics of Organizational Life. Cambridge, MA: MIT Press.
Hunt, Jennifer C.
   1989 Psychoanalytic Aspects of Fieldwork. Sage University Paper Series on Qualitative Research Methods, 18. Newbury Park, CA: Sage Publications.
Klein, Melanie
   1946 Notes on Some Schizoid Mechanisms. In Envy and Gratitude and Other Works. Pp. 1–24. New York: Basic Books.
Koenigsberg, Richard A.
   1975 Hitler's Ideology: A Study in Psychoanalytic Sociology. New York: Library of Social Science.
   1977 The Psychoanalysis of Racism, Revolution and Nationalism. New York: The Library of Social Science.
Kohut, Heinz
   1972 Thoughts on Narcissism and Narcissistic Rage. The Psychoanalytic Study of the Child 27:360–400. New York: Quadrangle Press.
La Barre, Weston
   1972 The Ghost Dance: The Origins of Religion. New York: Dell.
   1978 The Clinic and the Field. In The Making of Psychological Anthropology. George D. Spindler, ed. Pp. 258–299. Berkeley, CA: University of California Press.
Larçon, Jean-Paul, and Roland Reitter
   1984 Corporate Imagery and Corporate Identity. In The Irrational Executive: Psychoanalytic Studies in Management. M. F. R. Kets DeVries, ed. Pp. 344–355. New York: International Universities Press.
Mitscherlich, Alexander, and Margarete Mitscherlich
   1975 The Inability to Mourn: Principles of Collective Behavior. New York: Grove Press.
Modell, Arnold H.
   1984 Psychoanalysis in a New Context. Madison, CT: International Universities Press.
Nedelmann, Carl
   1986 A Psychoanalytical View of the Nuclear Threat—From the Angle of the German Sense of Political Inferiority. Psychoanalytic Inquiry 6(2):287–302.
Ogden, Thomas H.
   1989 The Primitive Edge of Experience. Northvale, NJ: Jason Aronson.
Owen, Harrison
   1986 Griefwork in Organizations. The Foresight Journal 1(1):1–14.
Pollock, George H.
   1977 The Mourning Process and Creative Organizational Change. Journal of the American Psychoanalytic Association 25:3–34.
Scott-Stevens, Susan
   1988 The Holistic Anthropologist: A Case Study of a Consultancy at a Western New Mexico Uranium Mine. High Plains Applied Anthropologist 8(1):3–32.
Searles, Harold F.
   1975 The Patient as Therapist to His Analayst. In Tactics and Techniques in Psychoanalytic Therapy, Volume 2: Countertransference. Peter L. Giovacchini, ed. Pp. 95–151. Northvale, NJ: Jason Aronson.

Stein, Howard F.
  1986   Unconscious Factors in Organizational Decision-Making: A Case Study from Medicine. Organization Development Journal 4(2):21-24.
  1987a Developmental Time, Cultural Space: Studies in Psychogeography. Norman, OK: University of Oklahoma Press.
  1987b Encompassing Systems: Implicatons for Citizen Diplomacy. Journal of Humanistic Psychology 27(3):364-384.
  1988   Aggression, Grief-Work, and Organizational Development: Theory and Case Example. Organization Development Journal 6(1):22-28.
  1990a Adapting to Doom: The Group Psychology of an Organization Threatened with Cultural Extinction. Political Psychology 11(1):113-145.
  1990b New Bosses, Old Losses: A Brief Case Study in Organizational Culture. Organization Development Journal 8(2):1-5.
  1991   Metaphors of Organizational Trauma and Organizational Development: A Case Example. Organization Development Journal 9(4):22-30.
Stein, Howard F., and Robert F. Hill
  1977   The Ethnic Imperative: Exploring the New White Ethnic Movement. University Park, PA: The Pennsylvania State University Press.
Stein, Howard F., and William G. Niederland
  1989   Maps From the Mind: Readings in Psychogeography. Norman, OK: University of Oklahoma Press.
de Tocqueville, Alexis
  1945[1835]   Democracy in America. 2 vols. P. Bradley, ed. New York: Knopf.
Tombaugh, Jay R., and Louis P. White
  1990   Downsizing: An Empirical Assessment of Survivors' Perceptions in a Postlayoff Environment. Organization Development Journal 8(2):32-43.
Volkan, Vamik D.
  1981   Linking Objects and Linking Phenomena: A Study of the Forms, Symptoms, Metapsychology, and Therapy of Complicated Mourning. New York: International Universities Press.
  1988   The Need to Have Enemies and Allies: From Clinical Practice to International Relationships. Northvale, NJ: Jason Aronson.
Wangh, Martin
  1986   The Nuclear Threat: Its Impact on Psychoanalytic Conceptualizations. Psychoanalytic Inquiry 6(2):251-266.
Winnicott, Donald W.
  1965[1963]   Psychiatric Disorders in Terms of Infantile Maturational Processes. In The Maturational Processes and the Facilitating Environment. Pp. 230-241. New York: International Universities Press.

About the Contributors

Ann T. Jordan is an assistant professor of anthropology at the University of North Texas, in Denton, Texas. She conducts research in the field of organizational anthropology and is especially interested in organizational culture and in the ethics of business consulting. To pursue her interest in the development of this field, she has organized sessions at the American Anthropological Association Annual Meetings, the Academy of Management Annual Meetings, and elsewhere. She is especially interested in cross-disciplinary work involving anthropology, organizational behavior, and management. Her publications include a coedited volume (with Tomoko Homada), entitled *Cross-Cultural Management and Organizational Culture*, as well as articles on various aspects of her organizational research. Her other research interest is American Indian studies.

Jill Kleinberg is an assistant professor of international management and organizational behavior at the University of Kansas School of Business. She is a cultural anthropologist, and her current research focuses on Japanese firms in both Japan and the United States.

Kanu Kogod is president of Bridges in Organizations, Inc., a company that provides management consultation and training in cultural diversity, to organizations of all types. Since 1992 she has performed as a senior consultant for University Associates Consulting and Training Services, San Diego, and has been an adjunct professor in the Graduate School of Business Administration at American University, in Washington, DC. Her publications include *The Anthropology of Treatment Failure, The Cultural Component of Customer Services*, and *One Method for Managing in the Multicultural Hospital*. Pfeiffer and Co. published her *Leader's Guide, Managing Diversity*, and she appears as a subject-matter expert on a video (also entitled *Managing Diversity*) by CRM Films. In 1994, Dr. Kogod coauthored (along with Anthony Carnavale, Ph.D.) a Department of Labor publication entitled *Our American Advantage: An Inventory of Diversity Tools and Strategies.*

Nancy C. Morey earned a Ph.D. in anthropology from the University of Utah in 1975. Her anthropological work had been focused on lowland South American cultures, both historical and modern. Her dissertation was on the ethnohistory of the southeastern llanos of Colombia and the southwestern llanos of Venezuela. She taught anthropology at the University of Utah,

Western Illinois University, and the Instituto de Investigaciones Cientificas in Caracas, Venezuela. In 1986 she earned a Ph.D. in management from the University of Nebraska, with a dissertation on the use of anthropological participant observation in the study of organizations. Currently her interests are in environmental issues, particularly recycling and in the application of anthropological theory and methods to research in organizations.

Robert V. Morey received his Ph.D. in anthropology from the University of Pittsburgh in 1970. He has conducted fieldwork in Colombia, Mexico, Venezuela, and the rural United States. He has taught at the University of Pittsburgh at Titusville, University of Utah, and Western Illinois University. He retrained in marketing in the mid-1980s and is currently a professor of marketing at Western Illinois University. His interests include international marketing, consumer behavior, culture of consumption, and the destruction of traditional societies.

Howard F. Stein, Ph.D., is a professor in the Department of Family Medicine, University of Oklahoma Health Sciences Center, in Oklahoma City, Oklahoma, where he has taught medical behavioral science since 1978. Coeditor of *The Psychoanalytic Study of Society,* and former editor of *The Journal of Psychoanalytic Anthropology* (1980–1988), he is author of over 150 articles and chapters, and of 12 books. His most recent book is *Listening Deeply: An Approach to Understanding and Consulting with Organizational Cultures,* published in 1994 by Westview Press. He is currently writing a book with several colleagues on the longitudinal study of a hospital undergoing "downsizing." He is a member of several organizations, including the International Society for the Psychoanalytic Study of Organizations.

napa bulletins

Why are anthropologists joining together in local practitioner organizations? What do anthropologists in government agencies do? How does one set up and operate a research and consulting business?

These are some of the questions answered in recent issues of the NAPA Bulletin, a monograph series for practitioners in the social sciences published semiannually by the National Association for the Practice of Anthropology, a section of the American Anthropological Association.

The following issues are now available:

2 Business and Industrial Anthropology: An Overview
Marietta L. Baba
$4.50 (members), $6.00 (nonmembers)

4 Research and Consulting as a Business
Nancy Yaw Davis, Roger P. McConochie, and David R. Stevenson
$2.00 (members), $4.00 (nonmembers)

5 Mainstreaming Anthropology: Experiences in Government Employment
Karen J. Hanson, ed., John J. Conway, Jack Alexander, and H. Max Drake
$2.00 (members), $4.00 (nonmembers)

6 Bridges for Changing Times: Local Practitioner Organizations in American Anthropology
Linda A. Bennett
$2.00 (members), $4.00 (nonmembers)

7 Applied Anthropology and Public Servant: The Life and Work of Philleo Nash
Ruth H. Landman and Katherine Spencer Halpern, eds.
$2.00 (members), $4.00 (nonmembers)

8 Negotiating Ethnicity: The Impact of Anthropological Theory and Practice
Susan Emley Keefe, ed.
$2.00 (members), $4.00 (nonmembers)

9 Anthropology and Management Consulting: Forging a New Alliance
Maureen J. Giovannini and Lynne M. H. Rosansky
$6.00 (members), $7.50 (nonmembers)

10 Soundings: Rapid and Reliable Research Methods for Practicing Anthropologists
John van Willigen and Timothy L. Finan, eds.
$10.00 (members), $13.50 (nonmembers)

11 Double Vision: Anthropologists at Law
Randy Frances Kandel, ed.
$10.00 (members), $13.50 (nonmembers)

12 Electronic Technologies and Instruction: Tools, Users, and Power
Frank A. Dubinskas and James H. McDonald, eds.
$10.00 (members), $13.50 (nonmembers)

13 Race, Ethnicity, and Applied Bioanthropology
Claire C. Gordon, ed.
$10.00 (members), $13.50 (nonmembers)

14 Practicing Anthropology in Corporate America: Consulting on Organizational Culture
Ann T. Jordan, ed.
$10.00 (members), $13.50 (nonmembers)

Please include payment, in U.S. funds, with all orders.

American Anthropological Association
4350 North Fairfax Drive, Suite 640
Arlington, VA 22203

Printed and bound by CPI Group (UK) Ltd, Croydon, CR0 4YY

10/06/2025

14686704-0001